DID YOU KNOW

DIDYANO?

Animal Families of the Zoos & Aquariums

THIS BOOK BELONGS TO

FROM

DATE

BE AWARE AND CARE

Written and Illustrated by
Timothy D. Thomas

DIDYANO?

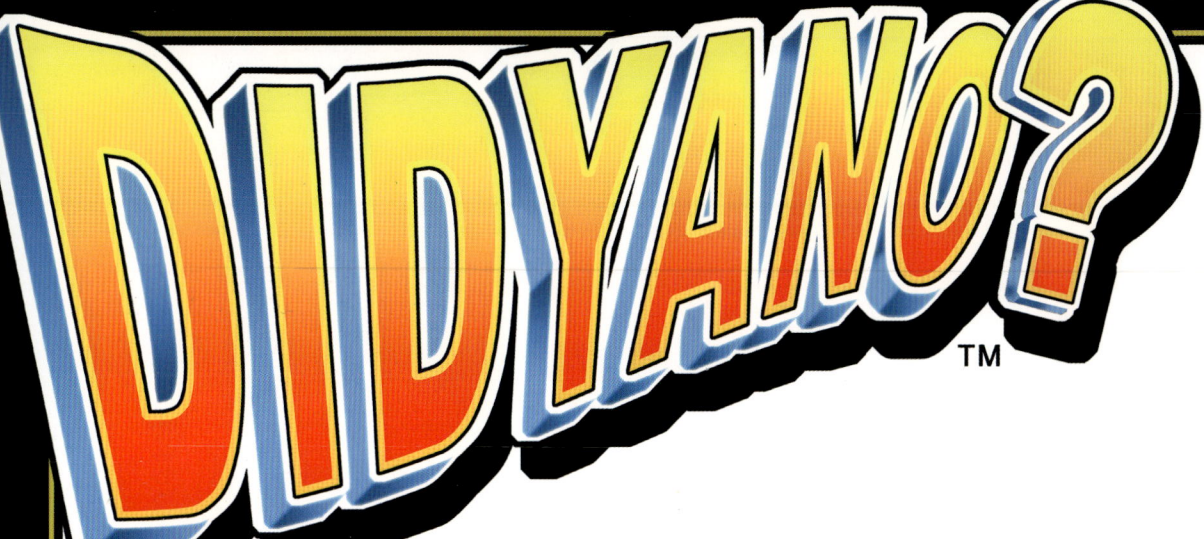

Animal Families of the Zoos & Aquariums

Written and Illustrated by
Timothy D. Thomas

ZOOS

Did you know the word *Zoo* derives from the Greek word *zwo* which means *animal*? The term *Zoo* is short for *Zoological Garden*. A *Zoological Garden* is a place or facility where living animals, especially wild ones, are kept within enclosures and displayed for people to see and admire.

The staff and workers of *Zoos* do more than just display wild animals.

- They watch and observe the animals for scientific research and study.
- They promote public education and awareness about different kinds of wild animals and their natural habitats.
- They observe living, eating and mating habits of the animals and how their babies are born and raised.
- They take care of sick, injured or orphaned animals.
- And much, much more!

Other names for *Zoos* are:
Zoological Gardens, *Zoological Parks*, or *Menageries*.

Thank you to the Association of Zoos and Aquariums (AZA) for their input and review of the contents of this book.

This book is dedicated to all the people who work to make visiting Zoos and Aquariums a pleasant experience for us all!

A Special Thank You To

Terri, Tanis, Mark, Vivian, Herb, Dewey, Kathy, Kevin, Gwen, Missi, Miki, Lydia, Ed and all my family & friends for their support!

Prepress by Mike.

Disclaimer:

DIDYANO? is an educational resource written for elementary age students. Thomas Expressions, LLC. does not cover all species in their entirety, nor are we capable of including all the latest scientific information and facts about the animals described. Though we edit our accounts for accuracy, we cannot guarantee all information in those accounts. While Thomas Expressions, LLC. 's staff and contributors provide reputable information, we cannot necessarily endorse the contents of references beyond our control.

U.S. Publisher Cataloging-in-Publication Data (Library of Congress Standards)

Thomas, Timothy D.

DIDYANO? – Animals Families of the Zoos & Aquariums

a. Author, Timothy D. Thomas
b. Illustrator, Timothy D. Thomas

[64] p. : col. Illustrated; 28.575 x 28.575 cm (DIDYANO? I)
Includes Text & Illustrations
Summary: Did you know? Animal Family Names, Fun Facts & Trivia.

ISBN 978-0-9771059-2-2

1. Animals 2. Animals – Pictorial works.
3. Animals-Miscellanea – Juvenile Literature.
4. Questions and Answers.
5. Aquariums, Public - Juvenile Literature.
6. Zoo Animals - Juvenile Literature.

I. Thomas, Timothy D.   II. Title.   III. Series   590 [JE]

Elementary Grade – Library Bound

© Copyright 2008 Thomas Expressions, LLC.
Panama City, Florida 32404
Published in the United States of America.
Printed in China through Colorcraft Ltd., Hong Kong.

ThomasExpressions.com,   Didyano.com & BeAwareAndCare.com

DIDYANO, DIDYANO?, DIDYANO.com,
Be Aware and Care, BeAwareAndCare.com,
Thomas Expressions and ThomasExpressions.com
are all registered trademarks of Thomas Expressions, LLC.,
and may not be used for any reasons unless by written permission
from the author and Thomas Expressions, LLC.
Thomas Expressions Publishing Company
is an imprint of Thomas Expressions, LLC.

DIDYANO?

PRIDE of LIONS
FAMILY: *FELIDAE*

BE AWARE AND CARE

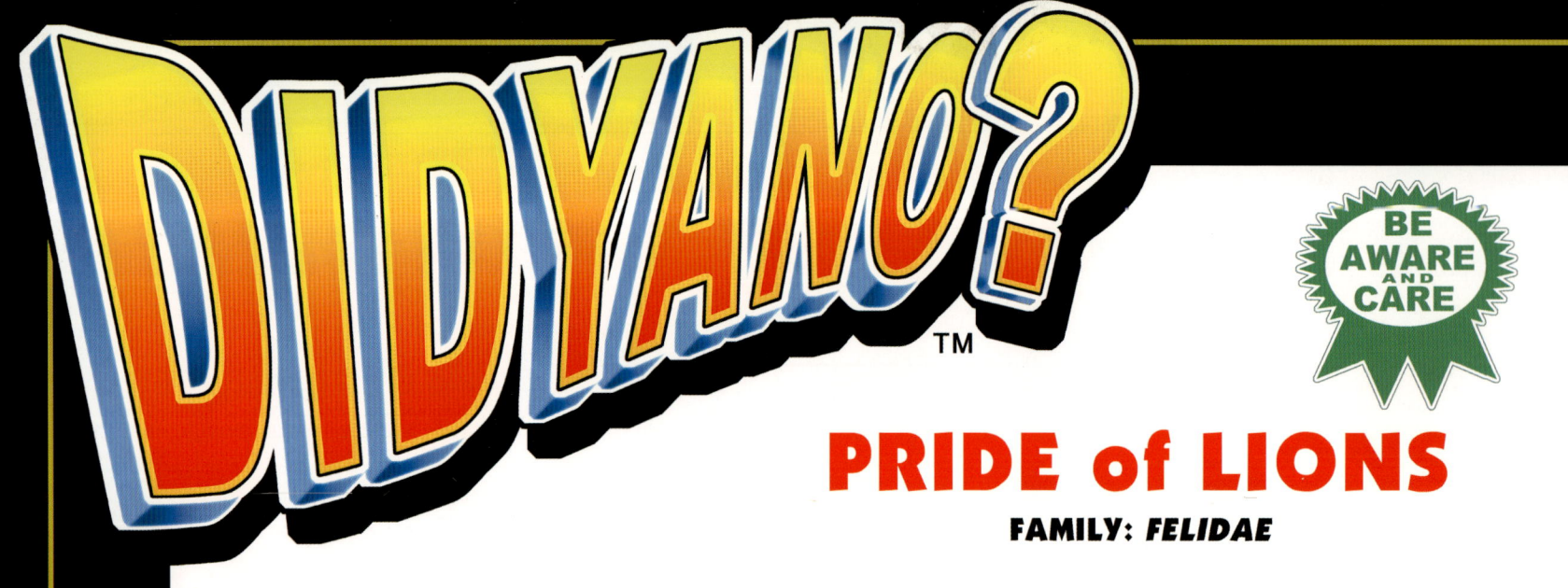

LIONS are large, strong, meat-eating cats that have a short, tan coat and a tufted tail. They live mainly in the grasslands of Africa, but can be found in China and India. **Lions** are known as *The King of Beasts*.

Did you know that **Lions** live in family groups of up to 30 individuals called a *pride*? A *pride* of **Lions** consists of a leader called the *dominate male*, related females, offspring and a small number of adult males. They are the only truly social cat species, and females in the *pride* are closely related. **Lions** appear to be quite lazy creatures and spend as much as 20 hours a day resting. **Lions** usually hunt during the day and prey upon mammals like antelope and zebra.

The *Swahili* word for **Lion** is *Simba*.

The male **Lion** is called a *Lion*. It is one of the largest of the cat family weighing in at more than 525 pounds and standing up to 4 feet tall. The male has a heavy coat of hair around the neck and shoulders called a *mane* which gradually darkens with age. Because of his dark *mane*, an old male is known as a **Black-Maned Lion**. The **Lion's** *mane* makes his body appear larger and more impressive than he really is, which helps to attract females and frightens off rival males.

The female **Lion** is called a *Lioness*. She and the other females do almost all of the hunting for the *pride*. A *Lioness* can give birth to a litter of one to four babies at a time. She is ferocious when defending her young. Sometimes, several *Lionesses* will team together to chase off a *predator* like a hyena or an aggressive male **Lion**.

A baby **Lion** is called a *Lionet*, *Whelp*, *Shelp*, or *Cub* and cannot *roar* until it reaches the age of two.

Other group names are: **Tribe**, **Sault**, or **Sowse**.

The sound a **Lion** makes is called a *Roar*.

People who are very brave and courageous are said to be *Lion-hearted* and if they're very strong they are said to be as *strong as a Lion*. However, if they are frightened all the time, then they are called *scaredy-cats*. To have the *Lion's share* of something means you have the most or biggest piece. It comes from the male **Lion's** habit of eating before the rest of the *pride* and devouring the most food.

Be Aware & Care
Habitat destruction, the loss of prey and unsustainable trophy hunting are pushing the Lion, one of the world's most feared predators, closer to extinction. You can show you care and help protect the Lions by making others aware why it is important to protect the lands they live on and to protect the animals the Lions prey upon to ensure the Lions survival.

DIDYANO? No two Lions have the same pattern of whiskers on their muzzles?

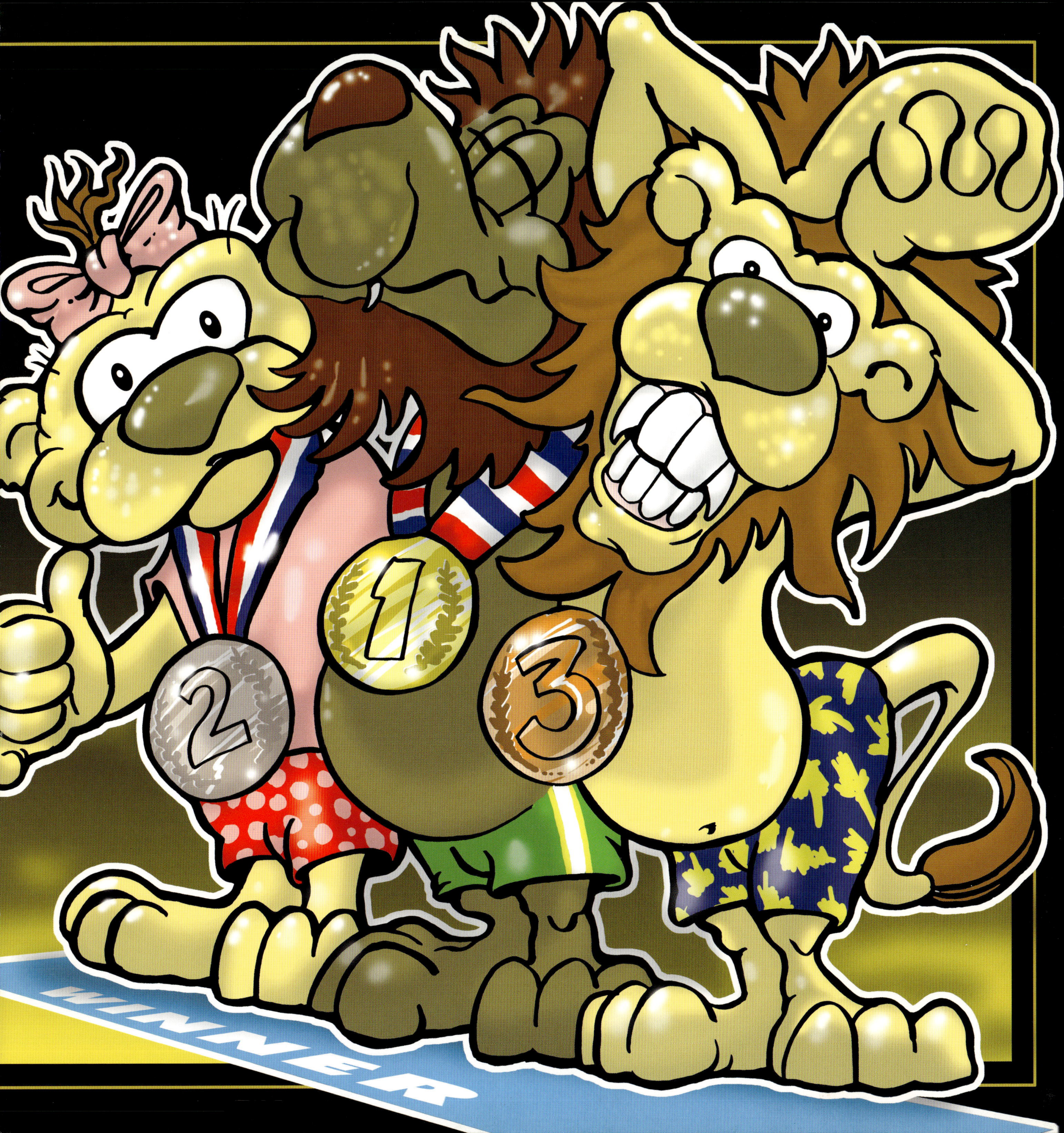
WINNER

DIDYANO?

BE AWARE AND CARE

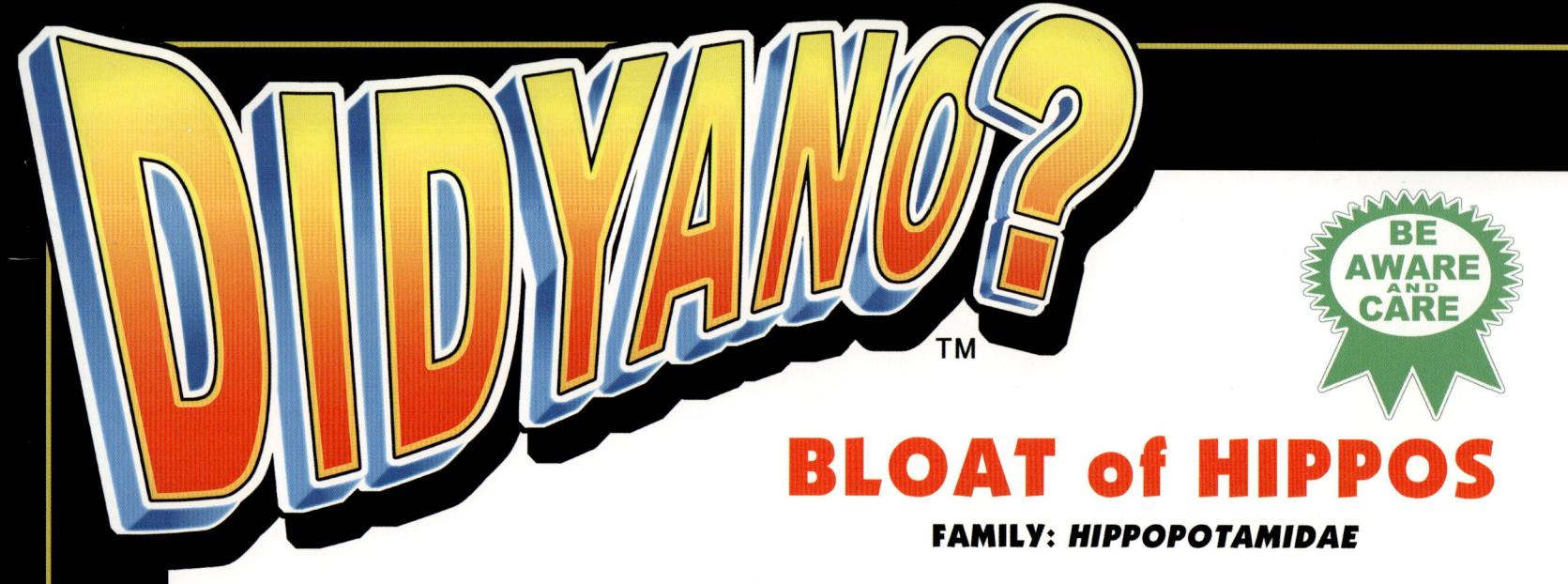

BLOAT of HIPPOS
FAMILY: *HIPPOPOTAMIDAE*

HIPPOS or **HIPPOPOTAMUSES** are large African animals that eat plants, live mostly in the water and have thick, almost hairless skin. They stand on four short legs and have webbed toes. **Hippos** have excellent hearing, sight, and smell. The name **Hippopotamus** comes from the Greek words **Hippos**, meaning *horse*, and **potamus**, meaning *river*. Though the **Hippo** spends most of its day in the water, it comes out at night to graze and can eat up to 100 pounds of vegetation in one night. The **Hippopotamus** is a **pachyderm** which means *thick skin*, and its skin is an inch and a half thick; so solid that most bullets cannot penetrate it. **Hippos** are not very friendly with each other and often fight.

Did you know **Hippos** live in a family called a *bloat*? As groups of **Hippos** enter areas of water such as streams or ponds they cause the waters in them to swell or *bloat*. **Hippos** are extremely territorial and males will search for the best territory along the shoreline and defend it. During warm weather **Hippos** secrete sweat which is pink or red called *blood sweat*. This substance not only cools them down, but also helps fight infections of the skin. **Hippos** are considered the most dangerous animal in Africa and have been known to attack and flip boats.

The *Swahili* word for **Hippo** is *Kiboko*.

The male **Hippo** is called a *Bull* and he can grow up to 12 feet long, 5 feet tall and can weigh up to 8,000 pounds. He has big **canine teeth** that continually grow from his broad, wide mouth and can reach lengths of up to 20 inches long.

The female **Hippo** is called a *Cow* and gives birth to her young underwater in the rivers and lakes where she lives. A female **Hippopotamus** will go off by herself to have her baby. She will stay away from the *bloat* for as long as a month before returning with her baby.

A baby **Hippo** is called a *Calf* and nurses underwater. When in the water a newborn *Calf* will often climb onto it's mother's back to rest. To protect her *Calf*, the mother **Hippo** may group together with other females to form a *nursery bloat*.

Other group names are: **Pod**, **Herd**, **Siege**, or **Huddle**.

The sound a **Hippo** makes is called a *Bellow* or a *Wheeze*. **Hippos** are one of the noisiest animals in Africa.

Be Aware & Care
The most serious threat to the future of the Hippo is loss of habitat. There is usually no shortage of water for daytime retreats, except in times of serious drought, but there are reports of loss of grazing habitat to cultivation. You can show you care and help protect the Hippos by making others aware why it is important to protect land and waterways in which Hippos live, eat, and raise their young.

DIDYANO?
Hippos cannot swim or float?

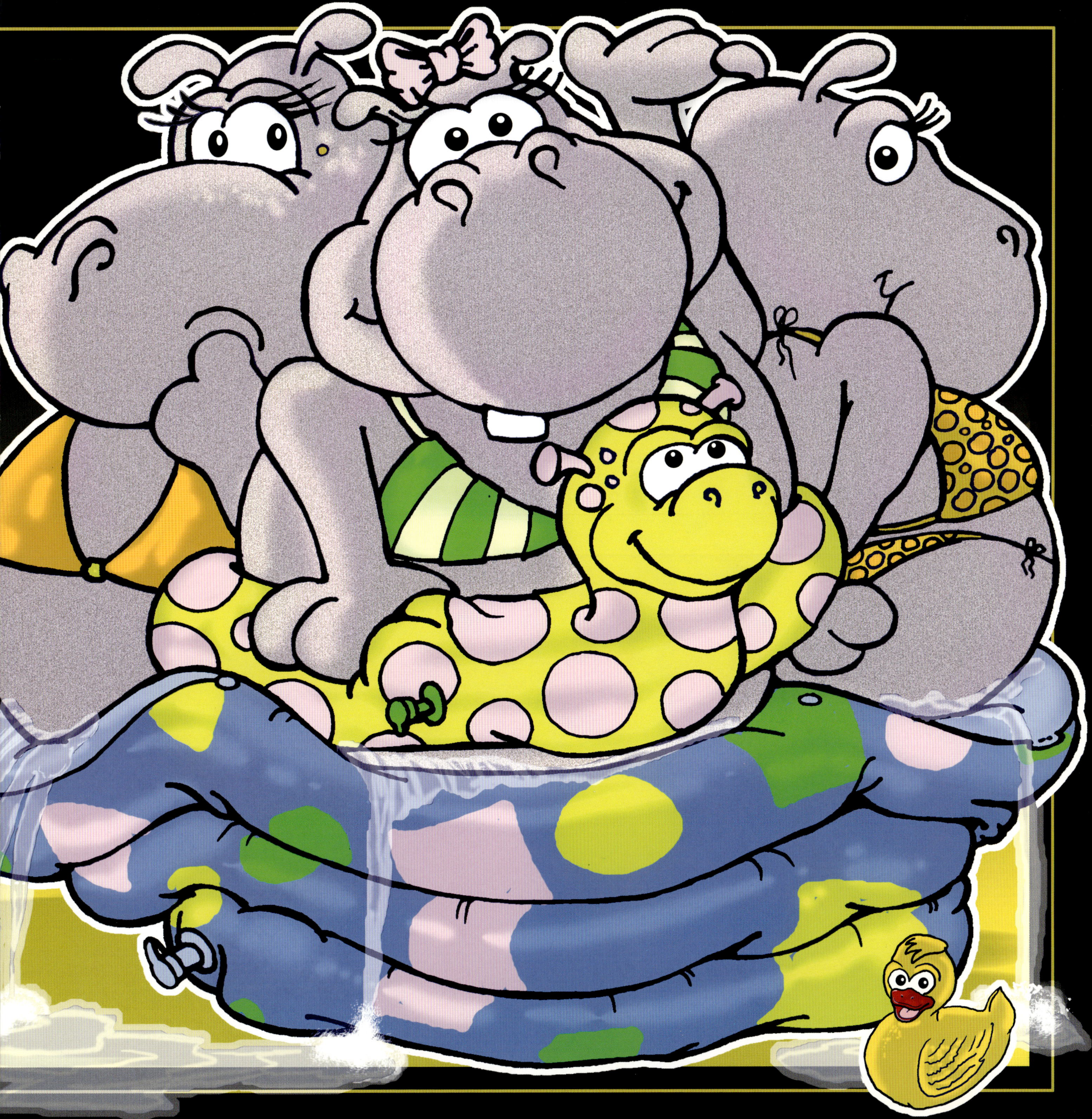

DIDYANO?

BAND of GORILLAS
FAMILY: *HOMINIDAE*

BE AWARE AND CARE

GORILLAS are the largest of the apes and are native to the forests of Africa. **Gorillas** have a stocky body and coarse, dark brown or black hair. **Gorillas** are the largest primates and part of a group called *Great Apes*. **Gorillas** are herbivores, eating fruits, leaves, roots and shoots. *Great Apes* walk by what is called *knuckle-walking*; they support their bulk on the knuckles of their hands, rather than the palms, like monkeys do. *Great Apes* also don't have tails.

Did you know **Gorillas** live in a family group called a *band*? A *band* is an organized social group of individuals living together cooperatively. Everyone has his or her place in a **Gorilla** *band*. The *dominant male* is the boss or the leader and is usually the most experienced and knowledgeable of the **Gorillas**. Often, he has younger or less dominant males in the *band*, who act as guards or sentries, to protect the group or bring up the rear when the *band* travels.

The *Swahili* word for **Gorilla** is *Gorila* or *N'gagi*.

The male **Gorilla** is called a *Boar*, *Black Jack*, or a *Silverback*. The band is lead by a *dominate male* called a *Silverback.* This refers to the silver-colored hair covering the back, which occurs when he's about 10-12 years old. He is sometimes twice as big as the females in his *band* or *harem*. A *Silverback Gorilla* can eat as much as 40 pounds of food each day.

The female **Gorilla** is called a *Sow*. When a *Sow* has a baby, her ranking in the band usually increases and females without babies are generally the lowest ranking members.

A baby **Gorilla** is called a *Suckling* or an *Infant*. **Gorilla** babies are helpless at birth, so they get rides by clinging to their mothers. When the group is not traveling, *Infants* are very active, spending much of their waking hours playing.

Other group names are: **Troop**, **Shrewdness**, **Family**, **Cartload**, or **Tribe**.

The sound a **Gorilla** makes is called *Grunting* or *Smacking*.

If your parents or teachers say you *act like an Ape*, it means you behave badly, wildly or foolishly.

Be Aware & Care
Hunting and poaching are the leading threats to Gorilla populations throughout Africa. Their survival is threatened by habitat destruction caused by agriculture and logging. You can show you care and help protect the Gorillas by making others aware why it important to protect the Gorilla and its mountain homeland.

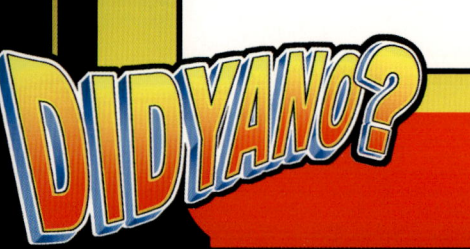

No two Gorilla noses are alike?

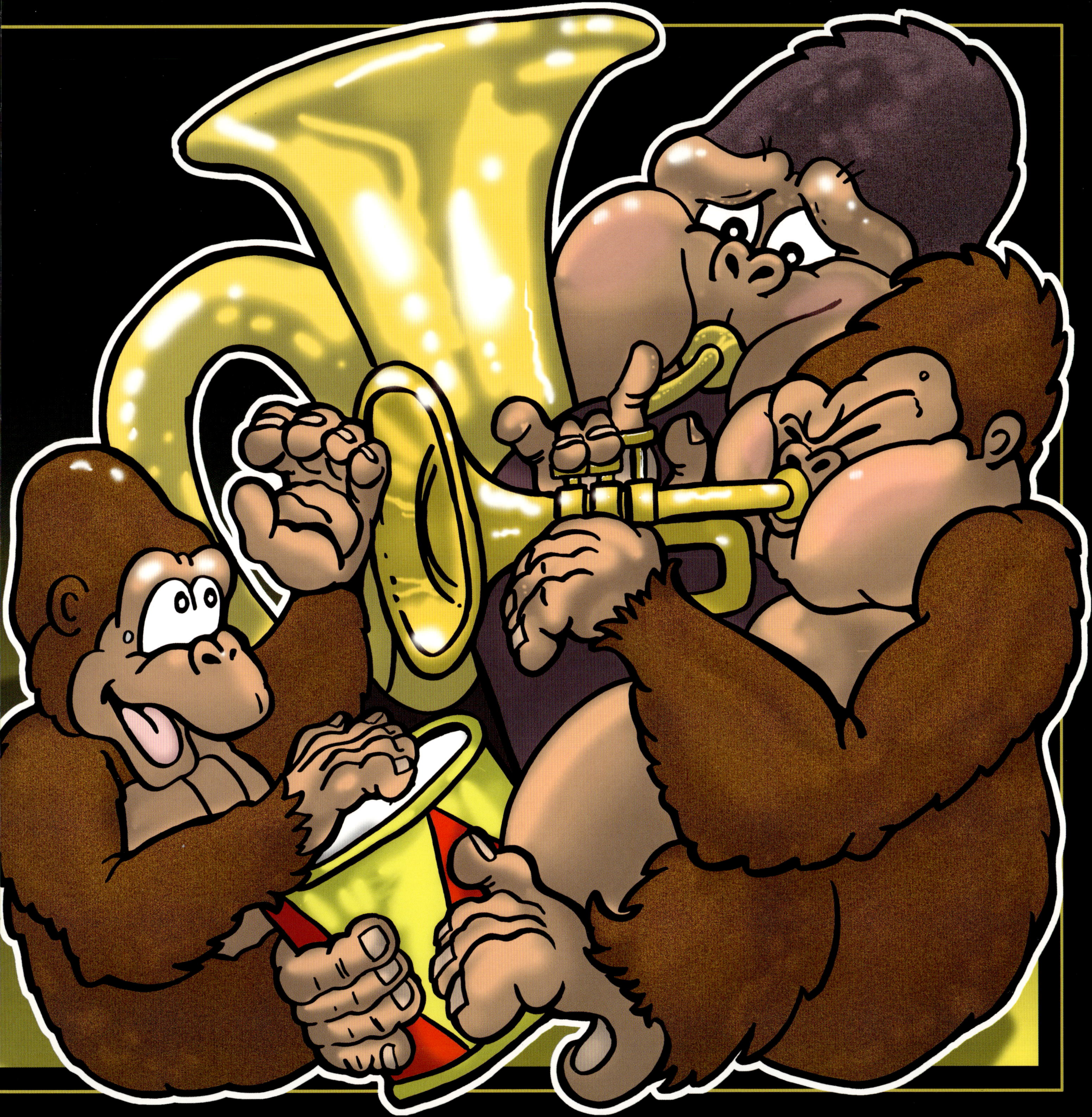

DIDYANO?

BE AWARE AND CARE

FLOAT of CROCODILES
FAMILY: *CROCODYLIDAE*

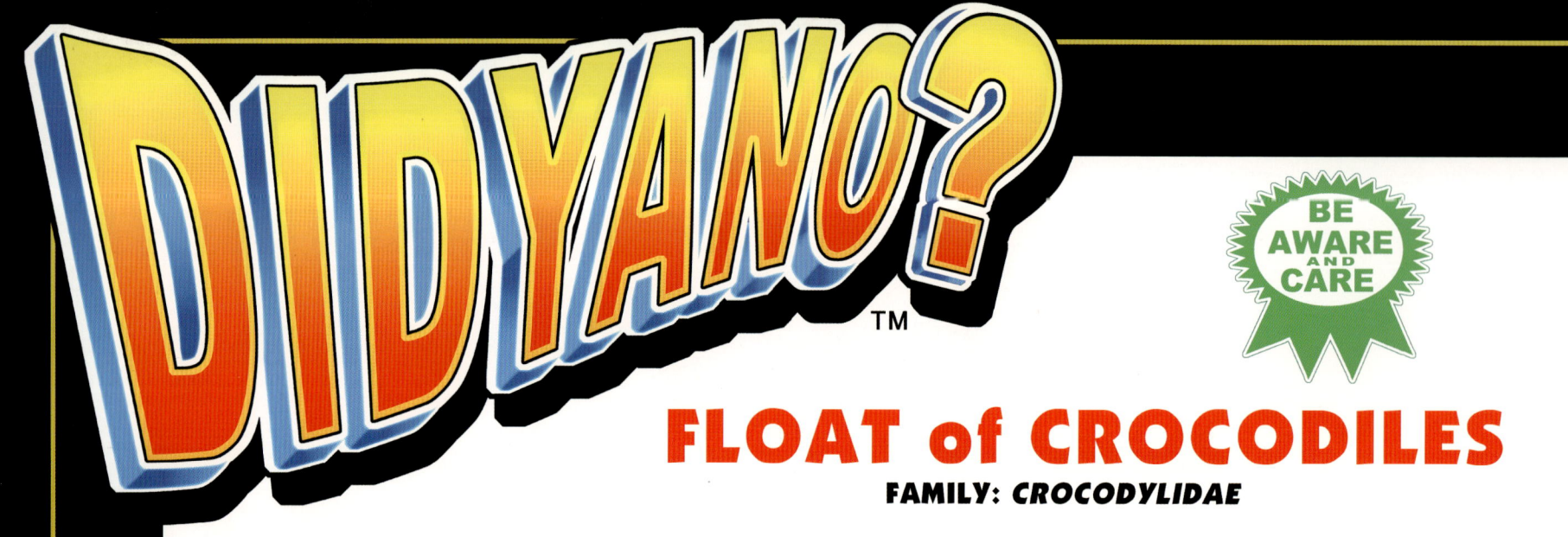

CROCODILES are large reptiles with four short legs and long muscular tails. They have a long snout with massive jaws and sharp teeth. Their bodies are covered with rough, bony plates called *osteoderms*. Large **Crocodiles** are capable of sudden bursts of speed from the water. They are so fast that their prey generally does not have time to react. The *Saltwater Crocodile* is the largest crocodilian and the largest living reptile.

Did you know a group of **Crocodiles** is called a *float*? They are *ambush hunters* hiding at the water's edge for prey. **Crocodiles** *float* just beneath the surface, waiting for fish or land animals to come close to them. The expression, to *cry crocodile tears*, or to shed fake tears, comes from a story of a **Crocodile** that moaned and sobbed like a person and lured a man into its reach. The **Crocodile** shed bitter tears over the death of the man after it ate him.

The *Swahili* word for **Crocodile** is *Mamba*.

The male **Crocodile** is called a *Bull*. Male *Saltwater Crocodiles* can weigh up to 2,000 pounds and reach lengths of 20 feet or more and will continue to grow all of their lives.

The female **Crocodile** is called a *Cow*. She builds a nest by pushing plants and soil into a mound near the water and will swim about it guarding the 30-40 eggs from predators. She takes very good care of her babies. **Crocodile** mothers are one of the few reptiles that care for their young until they are old enough to be on their own.

A baby **Crocodile** is called a *Crocklet*, *Hatchling* or *Nipper* and has an *egg tooth* on the end of its snout to open its leathery shell. If it has trouble breaking the shell open on its own, Mom may help by gently biting the egg. The little *Nippers* will ride in mom's mouth from the nest to the water where she will look after them for the next year.

Other family group names are: **Bask**, **Nest**, or **Congregation**.

The sound a baby **Crocodile** makes is called a *Grunt* or *Bark*.

The **Crocodile Hunter** was a title given to an Australian wildlife expert and television personality, *Steve Erwin*. (FEB 22, 1962 – SEP 4, 2006) He and his wife, *Terri Irwin*, co-owned and operated the **Australia Zoo**, in **Beerwah**, **Queensland**.

Be Aware & Care
The primary threat to Crocodiles is humans. While illegal poaching is no longer the primary problem, they are threatened by pollution, over hunting, and drowning in fishing nets. You can show you care and help protect Crocodiles by making others aware why it is important to protect the waters and nesting sites of these magnificent animals.

A Crocodile cannot stick out its tongue?

Crocodile Float

2 Scoops of Vanilla Ice Cream

2 Scoops of Mint Chocolate Ice Cream

Ginger Ale

Chocolate Syrup Topping

Two Crocodiles and a Cherry

DIDYANO?™

BE AWARE AND CARE

PARADE of ELEPHANTS
FAMILY: *ELEPHANTIDAE*

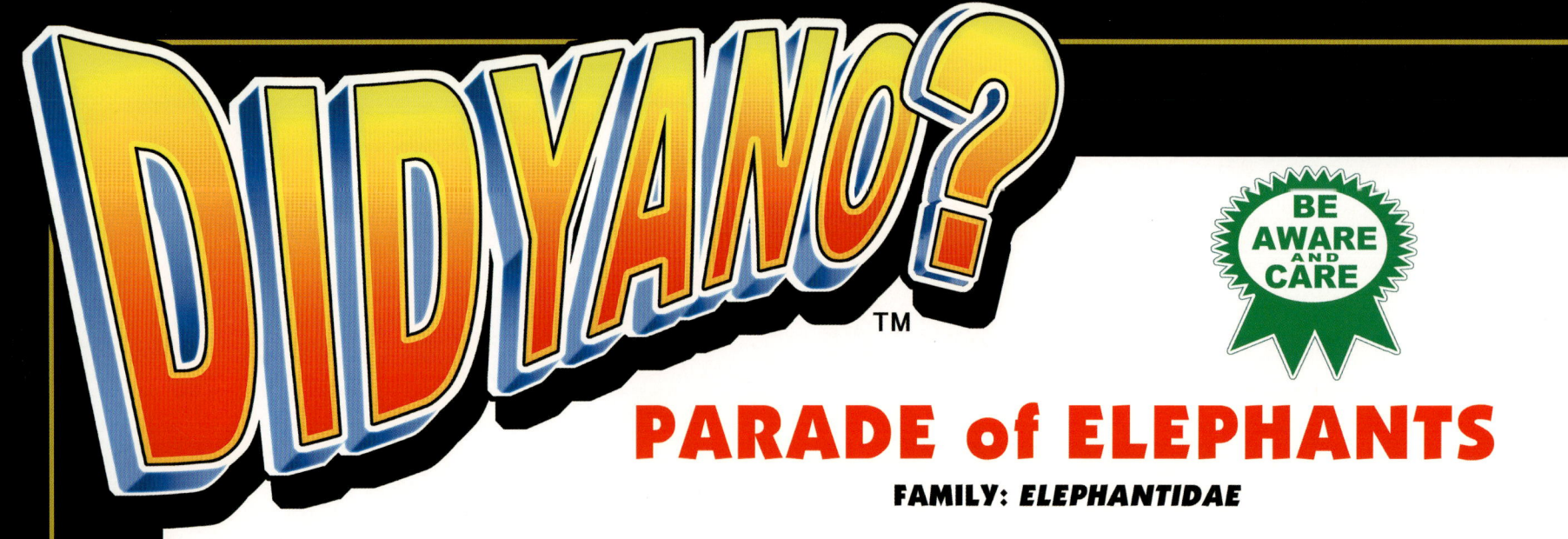

ELEPHANTS are large, plant-eating mammals of South-central Asia and Africa. They have thick, almost hairless skin, a long and flexible *trunk*, large fan-shaped ears and long curved *tusks*. *Tusks* are teeth made of *ivory* and **Elephants** use them for defense, digging, and for carrying things around. According to biologists, **Elephant** *trunks* may have over forty thousand individual muscles in it, making it sensitive enough to pick up a single blade of grass, yet strong enough to rip the branches off a tree. **Elephants** are the world's largest and heaviest land animals.

Did you know **Elephants** traveling in a group are called a *parade*? When they move from place to place, they form a procession line. As they march, they swing their *trunks* back-and-forth and trumpet loudly. Adult female **Elephants** and their young travel together, while adult males generally travel alone or in groups of their own.

The *Swahili* word for **Elephant** is *Tembo* or *Ndovu*.

The male **Elephant** is called a *Bull*. A fully grown *Bull African Elephant* can reach a height of over 10 feet and weigh as much as 15,000 pounds. He eats about 300 pounds of plants a day.

The female **Elephant** is called a *Cow* or *Koomkie* and is pregnant for almost 2 years. Both male and female *African Elephants* have large *tusks* that can reach over 10 feet in length and weigh over 200 pounds.

A baby **Elephant** is called a *Calf* and can weigh over 200 pounds at birth. The *Calf* has a short trunk, long tail and is very hairy. The *Calf* is born nearly blind and at first relies, almost completely, on its *trunk* to discover the world around it.

Other family group names are: **Herd**, **Host**, **Flock**, or **Memory**.

The sound an **Elephant** makes is called *Trumpeting*. It can also make low rumbling calls that can be heard by other **Elephants** 5 miles away.

It is said that an *Elephant never forgets*, so to have a *memory like an Elephant* means your memory is very good. Some people are said to live or work in an **Ivory Tower**, meaning in a very special place.

Be Aware & Care
Elephants face a range of threats including habitat loss and poaching. You can show you care and help protect the Elephants by making others aware that poaching is illegal and why it is important not to purchase items made from Elephant ivory. Also, Elephants cannot hide, and it takes many years for an elephant to grow and reproduce.

DIDYANO?
Elephants have four knees and can't jump?

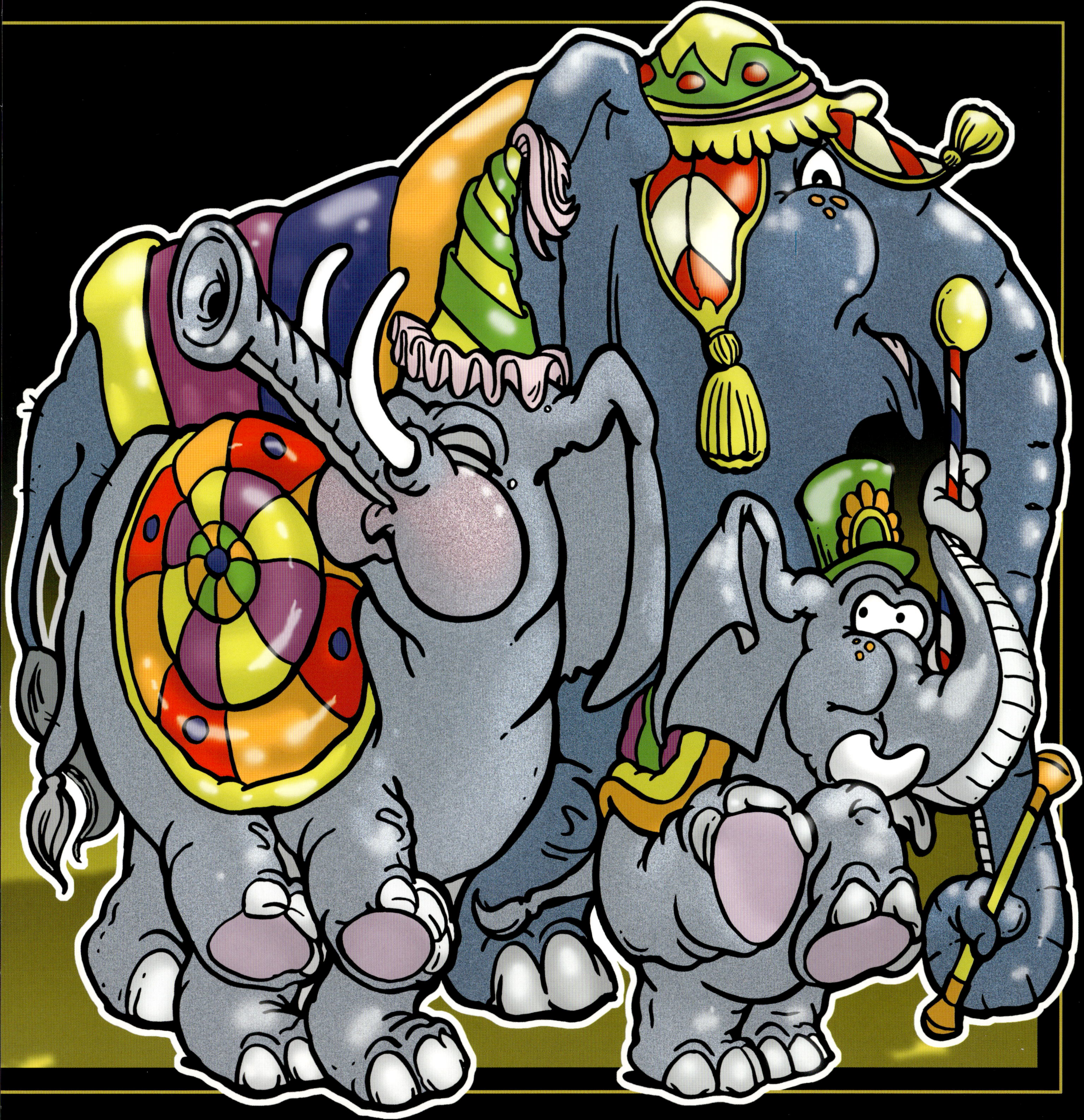

DIDYANO?

BE AWARE AND CARE

SLEUTH of PANDAS
FAMILY: *URSIDAE*

PANDAS are rare mammals that live in the mountains of China and Tibet, having woolly fur with distinctive black and white markings. The *Giant Panda* has a body typical of bears. It has black fur on its ears, eye patches, muzzle, legs, and shoulders. The rest of the animal's coat is white. Under the *Giant Pandas'* black fur, their skin is black and under the white fur, the skin is pink. Pandas are also called *The Giant Pandas* or *Panda Bears*.

Did you know Pandas live in a family group called a *sleuth*? The word *sleuth* means to *track down like a blood hound or a detective*. Since all bears forage for their food, they are constantly moving, smelling and looking for clues as to where their next meal may be. Bamboo is nearly 100% of the Pandas' diet. They have five fingers on their hand **PLUS** a thumb.

There are two *Chinese* words for Panda;
Huaxiong which means a *cat-like bear* and Maoxiong which means a *bear-like cat*.

The male Panda is called a *Boar* or *He-Bear*. Fully grown he can reach the height of 5-6 feet. An adult weighs about 275 pounds.

The female Panda is called a *Sow*, *Ursa*, or *She-Bear*. She plays with her baby by rolling and wrestling around with it.

A baby Panda is called a *Cub*. When the *Cub* is first born, it is pink, furless, blind, and is only the size of a stick of butter.

Other family group names are: Sloth, Slought, or Maul.

The sound a Giant Panda makes is called a *Bleat*, like a lamb or a goat kid.

If you are prepared for anything you would be *Loaded for Bear*. Pandas eat up to 85 pounds of bamboo a day. So, to be *Hungry as a Bear* means you are nearly starving! Can you imagine eating an 80 pound salad? Hopefully, your Mom doesn't make you eat that many veggies!

Some grouchy old-men have been said to be *Gruff as a Bear*, but most of them turn out to be *big ole Teddy Bears*.

Be Aware & Care
Pandas are found only in China, one of the world's most populated countries. The Giant Pandas clings to survival, facing habitat fragmentation and poaching as its greatest threats. You can show you care and help protect the Pandas by making others aware they are one of the most endangered animals in the world.

DIDYANO? Pandas spend 16 hrs a day eating bamboo?

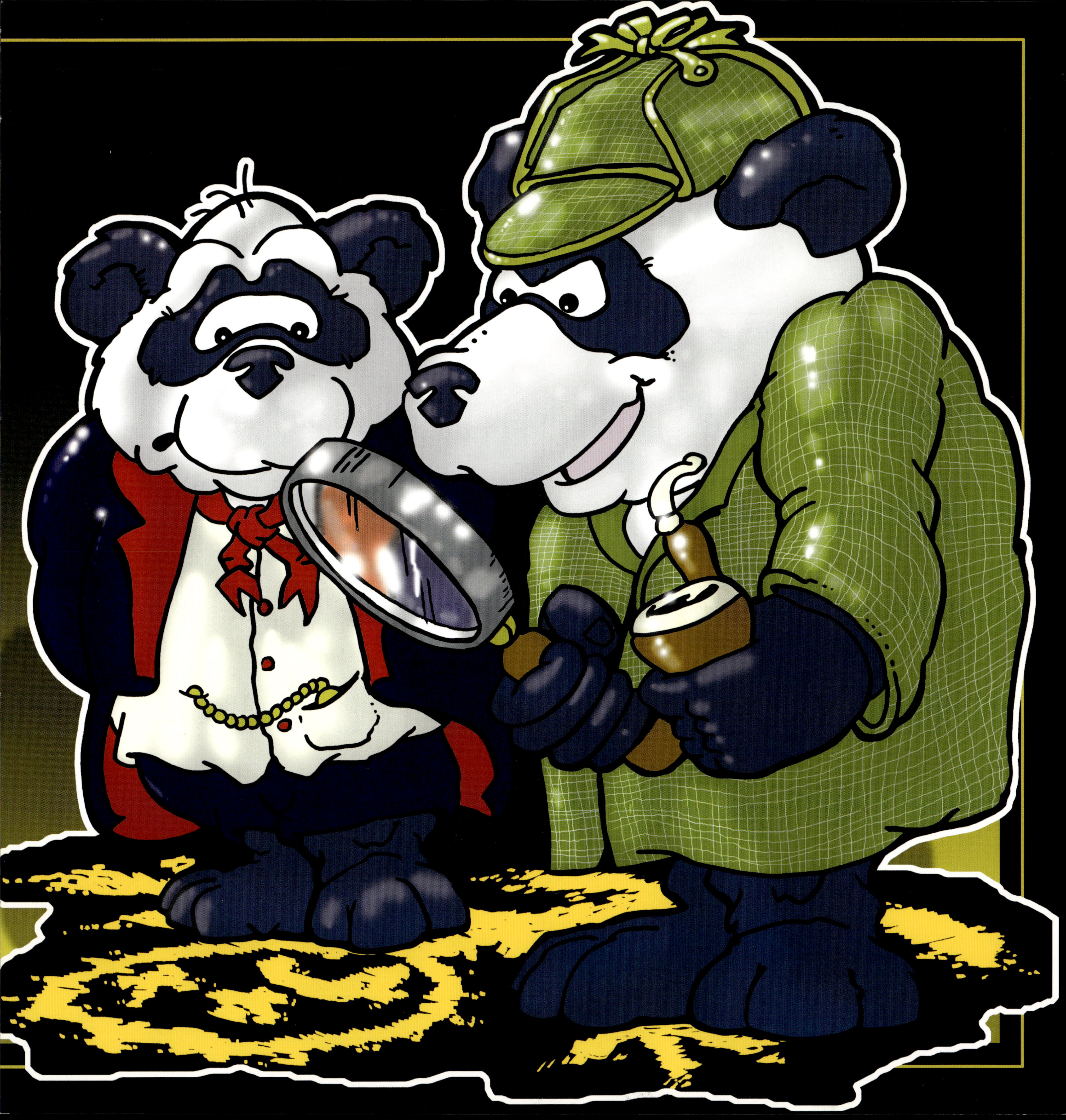

DIDYANO?

CLAN of HYENA
FAMILY: *HYAENIDAE*

BE AWARE AND CARE

HYENAS or **HYAENAS** are nighttime hunters and *scavengers* of Africa and Southern Asia. They look similar to dogs and feed chiefly on meat and dead animals. The *Spotted Hyenas* have powerful jaws, relatively short hind limbs, and coarse hair. Their *manes* on the top of their necks stand erect when they are frightened.

***Did you know** Spotted Hyenas* live in a family called a *clan*? A *clan* usually refers to a group of people of common descent, but holds true to **Hyenas** as well. All the members in the *clan* are closely related. They are mothers, sisters, aunts and daughters and are led by a *dominant female*. Related males group together to themselves or run off and find other *clans*. With their extremely strong jaws, **Hyenas** can easily crush large bones which they are able to digest. They often devour all parts of their prey including skin, teeth, horns, and even hooves. Little evidence remains of their actual meals.

The *Swahili* word for **Hyena** is *Fisi*. The word **Bultungin** translates as - *I change myself into a Hyena* - and is the African equivalent to America's Werewolf myth.

The male **Spotted Hyena** is called a *Dog*. **Hyenas** see very well in the dark.

The female **Spotted Hyena** in charge of the *clan* is called the *matriarch*. The female **Hyenas** are generally larger than the males. Female **Hyenas** are wonderful moms. They take excellent care of their babies, and most **Hyenas** provide their young with milk for over one year.

A baby **Spotted Hyena** is called a *Cub*, *Whelp* or *Pup*. The *Pup* stays close to the den until it is old enough to go hunting.

Other family group names are: **Cackle** or **Sorority**.

The sound a **Hyena** makes is called a *Laugh* or *Cackle* that sometimes sounds like it is laughing or giggling.

Someone who laughs very loudly and heartily is said to *laugh like a Hyena*. Of course **Hyenas** don't laugh like a human, but it has been said that their barks and calls do resemble the sound of laughter. This led to the belief in some African tribes that the **Hyenas** could imitate human voices and lure victims out by calling their names.

Be Aware & Care
Like most wild animals, the most serious threat to the Spotted Hyena is loss of habitat. Development, especially cattle farming, is constantly destroying the habitat of Hyenas and many other animals. You can show you care and help protect the Hyenas by making others aware why it is important to protect them and the lands they live and hunts on.

A Hyena can eat up to 1/3 its body weight in meat and bone?

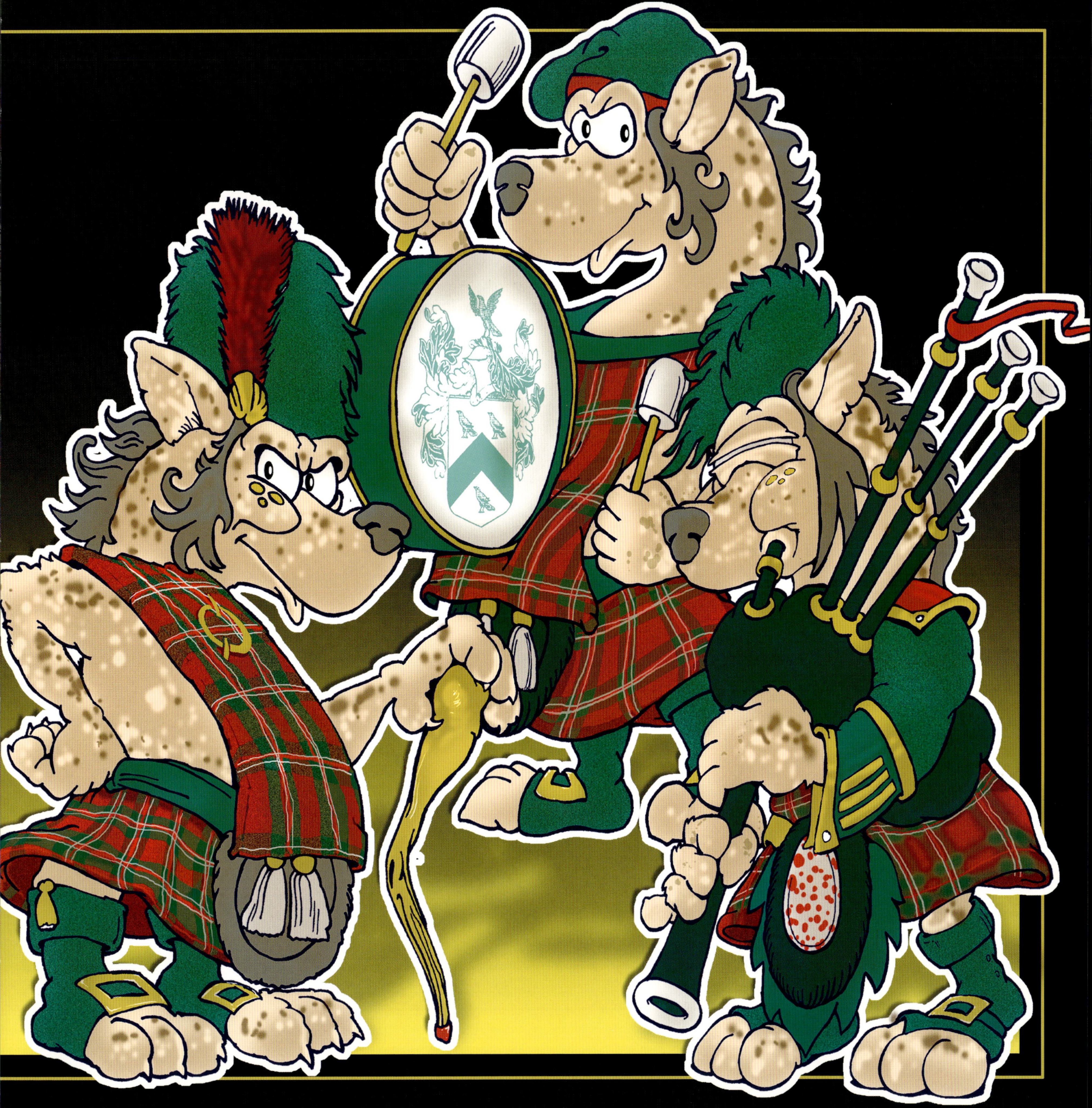

DIDYANO?

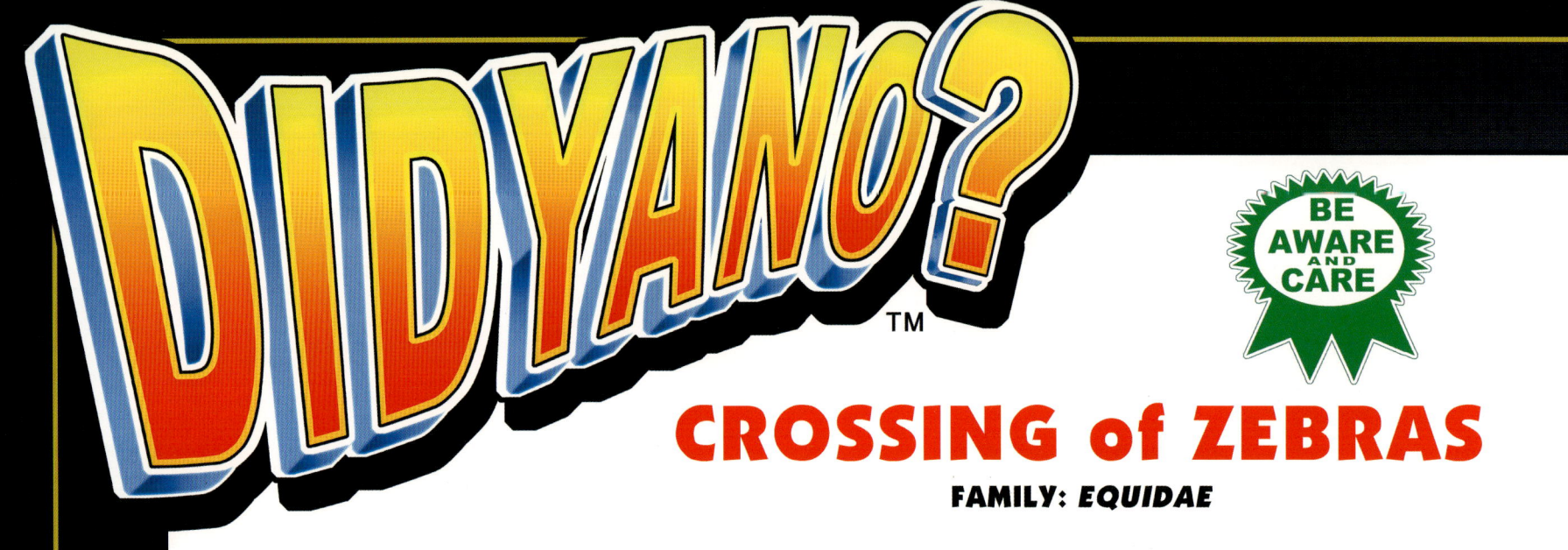

BE AWARE AND CARE

CROSSING of ZEBRAS
FAMILY: *EQUIDAE*

ZEBRAS are African horses. They are white-haired animals with black stripes and no two have exactly the same stripe pattern. The **Zebras'** skin under their fur is black. **Zebras** have erect *manes* standing straight up on their necks and large dark eyes that can see very well at night. They have a keen sense of smell and are capable of running 40 mph.

Did you know **Zebras** travel in a group called a ***crossing***? They are constantly moving across the plains, ***crossing*** from field to field, looking for grass to graze on. They usually need to drink every day, so they do not wander far from waterholes. **Zebras** take mud and dirt baths to get clean and rid themselves of ticks and flies. They communicate with each other through sounds and facial expressions. **Zebras** often greet each other with a wide toothy grin or smile.

The *Swahili* word for **Zebra** is *Punda Milia*.

The male **Zebra** is called a *Stallion*. He stands 4-5 feet at the shoulders and weighs between 660 - 900 pounds.

The female **Zebra** is called a *Mare* and may give birth to one baby every 12 months. She nurses her young for a full year.

A baby **Zebra** is called a *Colt* or *Foal* and is able to stand, walk, and suckle shortly after it is born. A **Zebra** baby is white and brown instead of white and black at birth.

Other family group names are: **Zeal**, **Herd**, **Cohorts**, or **Stripe**.

The sound a **Zebra** makes is called a *Whuffling*.

If someone you know can talk you into doing things you wouldn't normally do, they are said to be able to ***talk the stripes off a Zebra***. ***If you hear hoof beats, think horses and not Zebras***, is a way of saying you should not be surprised and expect the obvious. If something is nearly impossible, the saying, ***It is easier for a Zebra to change its stripes***, might apply.

Be Aware & Care
Zebras were hunted mainly for their skins. They are still threatened by hunting and poaching, but primarily from habitat change due to farming. You can show you care and help protect the Zebra by making others aware why it is important to protect their grazing lands and waterholes. One subspecies of Zebra, the Quagga, is now extinct.

Zebras cannot see the color orange?

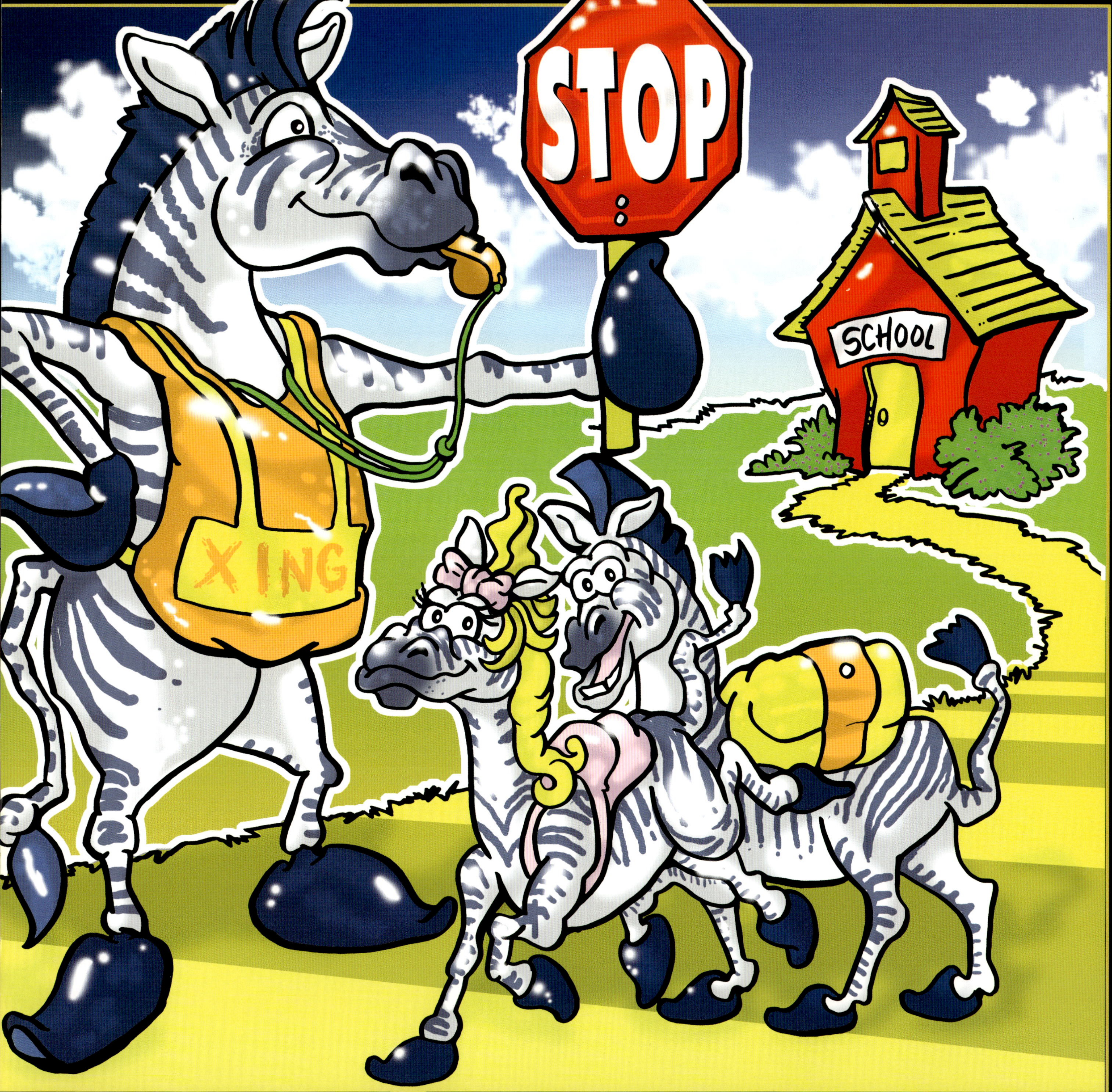
STOP
SCHOOL
XING

DIDYANO?

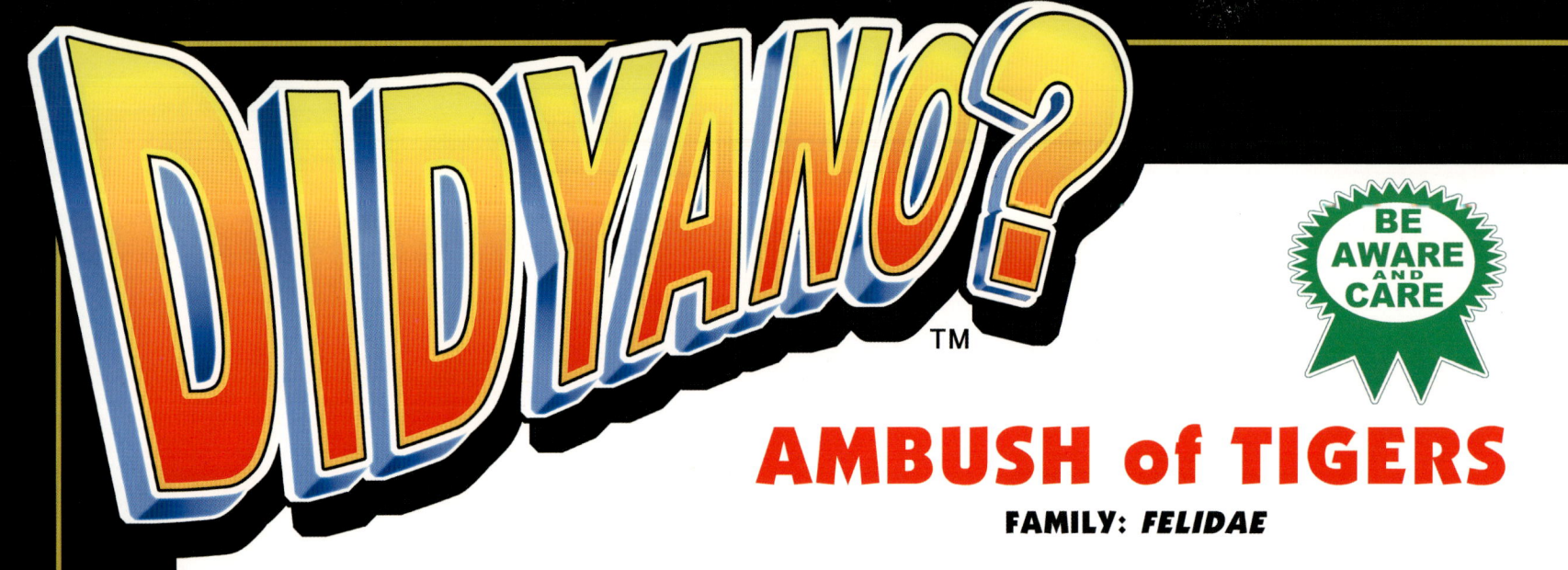

BE AWARE AND CARE

AMBUSH of TIGERS
FAMILY: *FELIDAE*

TIGERS are large, meat-eating cats that live in Asia, China, and India. They have tan or orange fur with black stripes. Their bellies are usually white. Like most cats their night-time vision is very good. They have round pupils and yellow irises. **Tigers** have retractable claws and the largest *canine teeth* of any meat eaters on land. There are also **White Tigers** with dark stripes and blue eyes.

Did you know that **Tigers** usually live alone, but sometimes gather in a group called an *ambush*? An *ambush* is when **Tigers** stalk their prey and hide in a concealed position in order to attack by surprise and stealth. Unlike most cats, **Tigers** are very good swimmers and like the water. They have striped skin, not just striped fur. The **Tigers'** *saliva* is very clean and comes in handy for cleaning their wounds.

The *Chinese* word for **Tiger** is *Hu*.

The male **Tiger** is called a *Tiger*. When fully grown he can reach the length of 11 feet from his nose to the tip of his tail and weigh up to 600 pounds.

The female **Tiger** is called a *Tigress* and gives birth to 2-4 young. She alone cares for them.

A baby **Tiger** is called a *Cub* or *Whelp*. It is born blind and is dependent on the mother for about 2 years until it can start hunting on its own.

Other family group names are: **Streak** or **Hide**.

The sound a **Tiger** makes is called a *Growl*; and **Tigers** don't purr.

If you have a *Tiger by the tail*, it means you are in a situation that has turned out to be much more difficult to control than you had expected.

Although the Lion is called the *King of Beasts*, all **Tigers** have a similar marking on their forehead, which resembles the Chinese symbol **Wang,** meaning *King*.

Be Aware & Care
While all surviving Tiger species are under formal protection, poaching, and habitat destruction continue to be threats. You can show you care and help protect the Tigers by making others aware that habitat destruction is the main threat to the existing Tiger population.

DIDYANO?
Tiger paw prints are called *pug marks*?

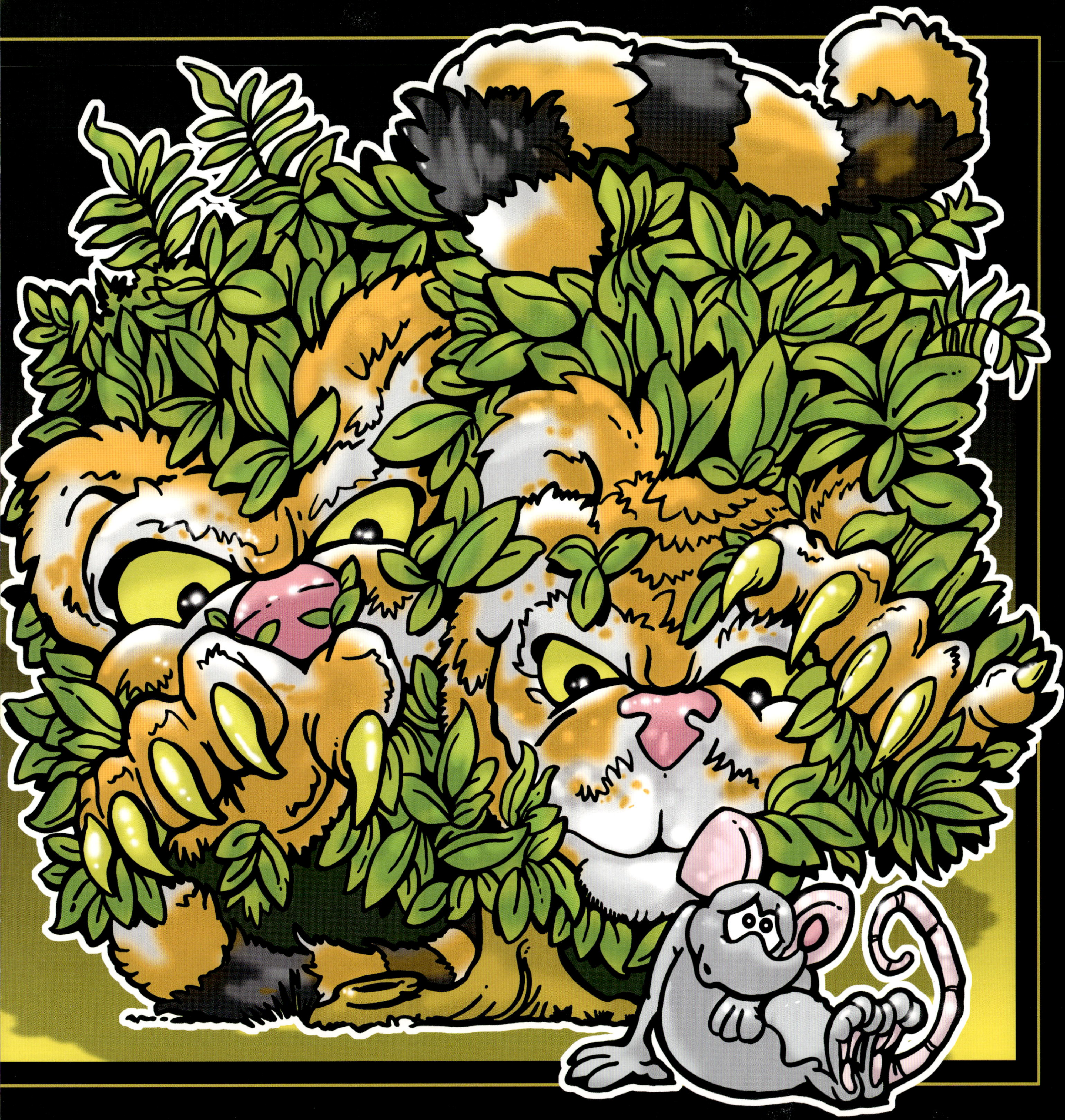

DIDYANO?

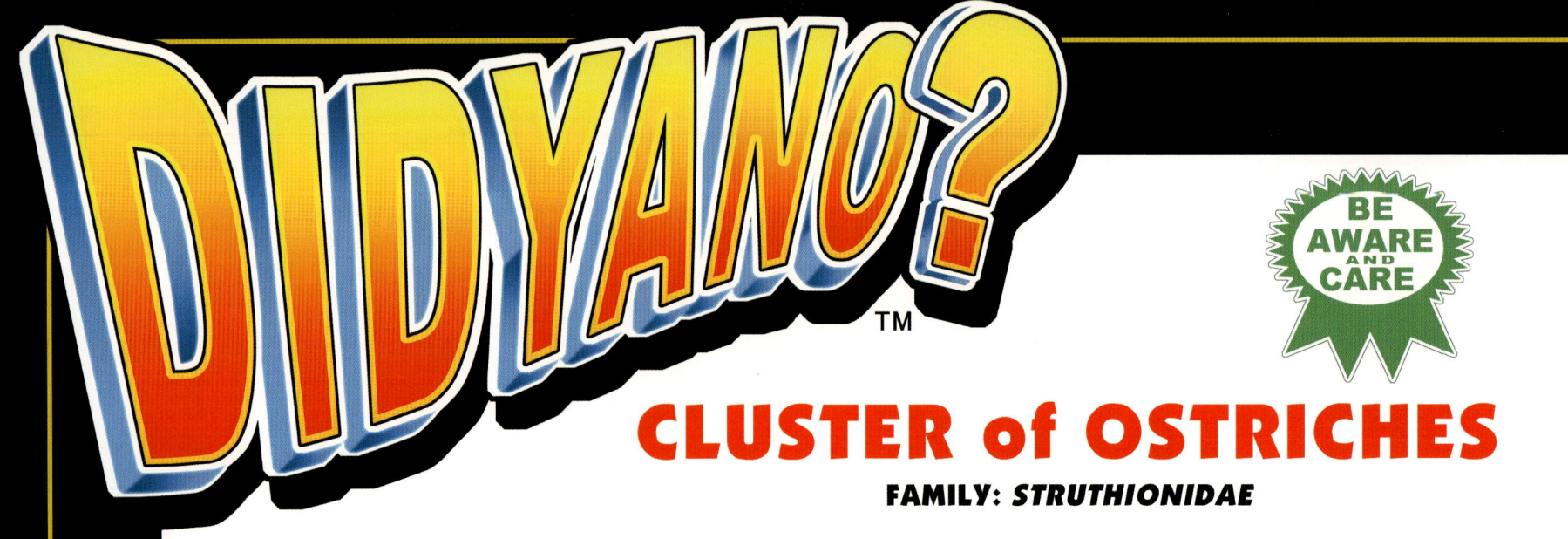

CLUSTER of OSTRICHES
FAMILY: *STRUTHIONIDAE*

BE AWARE AND CARE

OSTRICHES are the largest and heaviest of birds. They are swift-running, flightless, birds of Africa. They are characterized by a long, bare neck, small head, and two large feet. Ostriches have a four inch claw on each foot and their kick is powerful enough to kill a Lion. They have been known to run at sustained speeds of about 30 miles per hour.

Did you know Ostriches gather in a group called a *cluster*? Ostriches will *cluster* or gather into bunches for safety. The group usually consists of one male and 4-5 females. This male will form a strong relationship with one female called the *alpha female*. Ostriches don't have the strong, stiff wings and tails feathers of flying birds. Instead, they grow a soft *plumage* that acts as insulation against the harsh temperatures. The Ostriches' wings are very small and are used mainly for balance.

Ostriches shovel dirt and sand with their bills to dig large holes in the sand for their nests. All birds turn their eggs with their bills several times a day during the *incubation* period. So, from a distance it appears as though the Ostriches have their heads in the sand. Thus, the myth that Ostriches bury their heads in the sand when they are frightened is not true.

The *Swahili* word for Ostrich is *Mbuni*.

The male Ostrich is called a *Cock* or *Rooster*. It is the largest living bird in the world, standing 9 feet tall and weighing up to 345 pounds. Both the *alpha female* and the *Cock* will share in *incubating* the eggs and raising the young.

The female Ostrich is called a *Hen* and can lay 12-15 eggs in one *clutch*. Many *Hens* may lay eggs in the main nest, but it is usually the *alpha female* that will sit on the nest during the day and the *Cock* will sit on the nest during the night.

A baby Ostrich is called a *Chick*. It hatches from the world's largest bird egg. The egg can measure 7 inches across and weighs 3 pounds. One Ostrich egg can be as big as 24 chicken eggs.

Other family group names are: Flock or Brood

The sound an Ostrich makes is called a *Honk*.

Be Aware & Care
Although Ostriches are not globally threatened, they require strict protection. Ostrich farming has helped to conserve the wild populations. You can show you care and help protect the Ostriches by making others aware why it is important to protect them. Extensive hunting for feathers, meat, and skins coupled with overgrazing by domestic animals on their habitat has lead to concerns for the Ostrich and its future.

An Ostrich's eye is bigger than its brain?

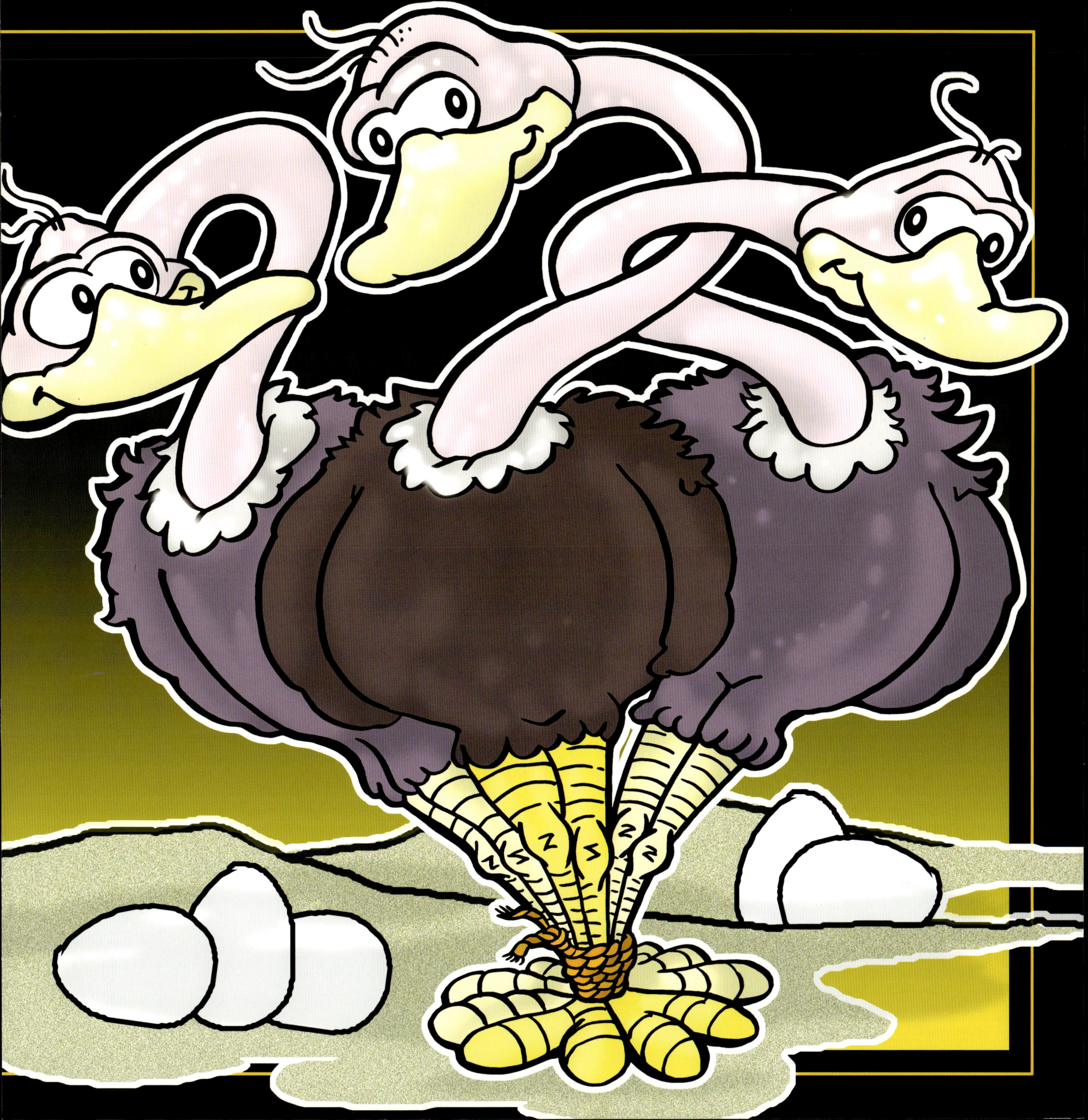

DIDYANO?

BE AWARE AND CARE

CRASH of RHINOS
FAMILY: *RHINOCEROTIDAE*

RHINOS or **RHINOCEROSES** are massive and powerful plant-eating animals that live in Southeast Asia and Africa. **Rhinoceros** means *nose horn*. They are brown or gray in color and have very thick skin. **Rhinos** have one or two distinctive horns that grow in the middle of their snouts. All **Rhinos** are *vegetarians*. In fact, *White Rhinos* can eat plants that are toxic to other animals. If it wasn't for the **Rhinos**, the African plains would be overtaken with these pesky weeds!

Did you know **Rhinos** sometimes live and travel in a group called a *crash*? Maybe they're called a *crash* because their size and strength gives them the ability to *crash* or plow though anything that is in their way. Or maybe, when it's time to sleep, **Rhinos** *crash* wherever they can find a comfortable place to rest. *White Rhinos* are basically solitary and territorial animals except for the mother and child unit and during the mating season. The *White Rhino* is also called the *square-lipped Rhinoceros* because of its broad, square, upper lip which it uses for grazing.

The *Swahili* word for **Rhino** is *Kifaru*.

The male *White Rhino* is called a *Bull* and can be over 6 feet tall at the shoulders and weigh from 3,000 to 5,000 pounds. The front horn is larger than the back horn and averages 24 – 59 inches in length. The *White Rhino* has a hump of muscle on its neck and shoulders to support a head that can weigh up to 1,000 pounds.

The female *White Rhino* is called a *Cow* and gives birth to one baby every 2-4 years.

A baby *White Rhino* is called a *Calf* and does not live on its own until it is about three years old.

Other family group names are: *Herd*

The sound a **Rhino** makes is called a *Snort*.

To take the bull by the horns means that you have the courage to step up and do it your way. You may even be considered *bullheaded*. Just be careful when you take a *Bull Rhino* by the horn. A *Bull Rhino* is *bullheaded* all the time.

Be Aware & Care
Poaching and habitat loss are the primary reasons for the Rhinos decline. You can show you care and help protect the Rhinos by making others aware it is illegal to purchase items made from the hides or horns of Rhinos. Explain to your family and friends why it is important to protect the lands that they live and feed on.

DIDYANO?
The horns of Rhinos are made of hair, not bone?

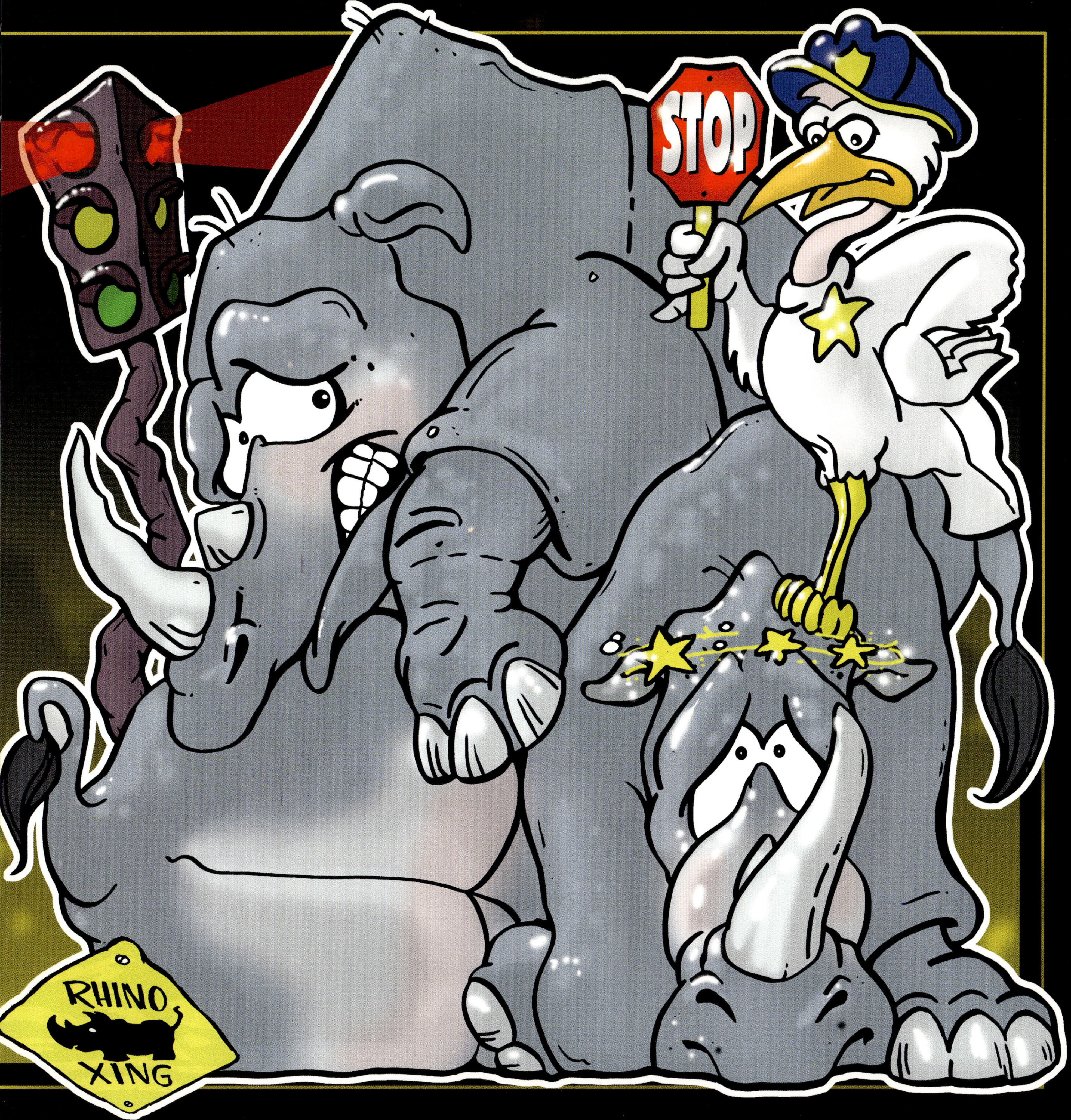
STOP
RHINO
XING

DIDYANO?

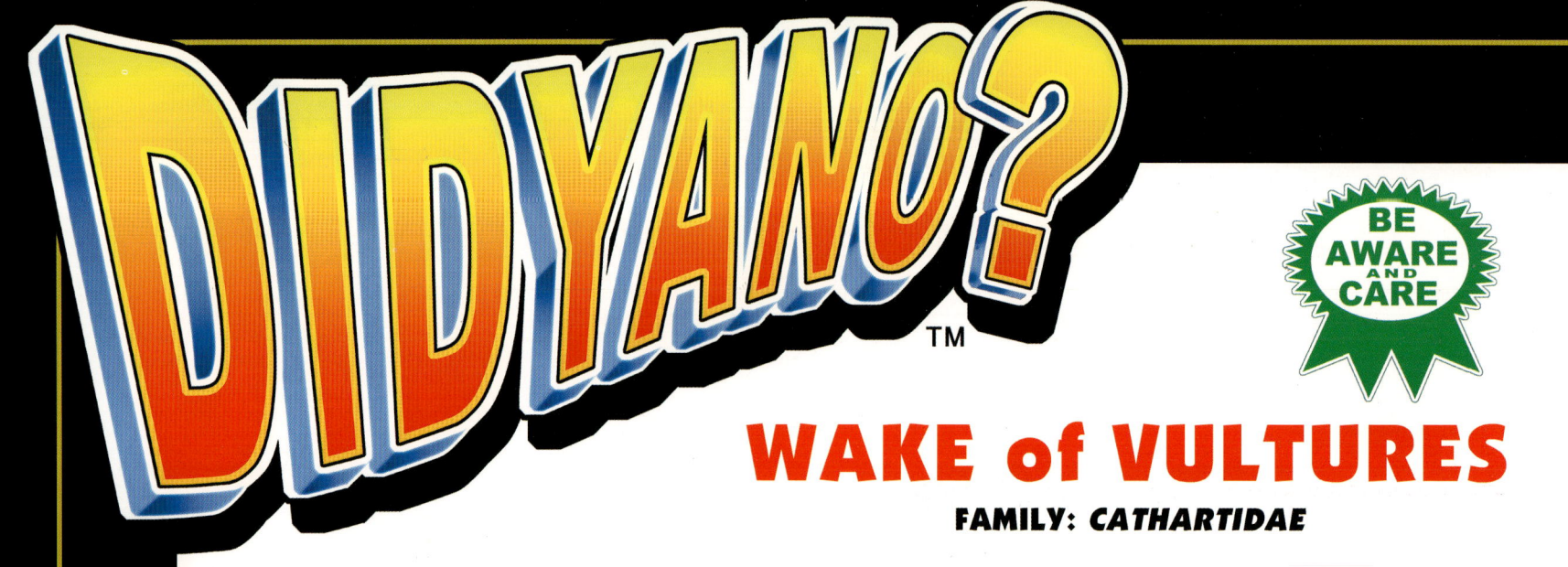

BE AWARE AND CARE

WAKE of VULTURES
FAMILY: *CATHARTIDAE*

VULTURES are large, short-tailed, solitary birds of prey. They are *scavengers* and have strong, *gastric juices* able to digest bones. **Vultures** feed on dead animals or *carrion*. They have hooked beaks which they use to tear flesh. Males and females are similar in size and coloration. Most have dark *plumage*, a short neck, weak feet, and a featherless head and neck. The word *buzzard* is loosely applied to most *raptors* that are not owls, eagles, falcons or kestrels, but may include the **Vultures** and condors.

Did you know that a group of perched **Vultures** is called a *wake*? A *wake* is a celebration of someone's life after they die and before they are buried. You can almost imagine a group of **Vultures** mourning over something dead with their heads hung low over a dying animal or *roadkill*. **Turkey Vultures** of America can locate their food using their acute sense of smell and keen eyesight. They have bald, red heads and dark feathers which resemble that of the **Wild Turkey**.

The **Latin** word for **Turkey Vulture** is ***Cathartes aura*** which means *cleansing breeze*.

The male **Vulture** is called a *Cock*. **Turkey Vultures** average 2 1/2 feet tall with a 6 foot wingspan. In spite of their large size, they only weigh between 2-4 pounds!

The female **Vulture** is called a *Hen* and usually lays one or two eggs in a *clutch*.

A baby **Vulture** is called a *Chick* and is white when it is born.

Other family group names are: **Flock**, **Committee**, or **Kettle**.

The sound a **Vulture** makes is called a *Chuff*.

The term *Buzzard Bait* is used to describe a dying or worthless animal. If they have only the slightest hope of living we say, *on a wing and a prayer*! *Old Buzzard* is a slang phrase for an old man or woman who is usually mean to younger people. *Woke up with the buzzards* is a saying about someone or something that is dead or about to die.

Be Aware & Care
Vultures serve an important function as nature's garbage collectors, helping to keep the environment clean of waste. You can show you care and help protect the Vultures by making others aware why it is important to protect their habitats. These habitats must be preserved and pollutants eliminated so these important birds are not lost.

Vultures can soar for hours with one beat of their wings?

HERE LIES
SEYMOUR
THE TOAD

HE DIDN'T
MAKE IT
ACROSS THE
ROAD

DIDYANO?

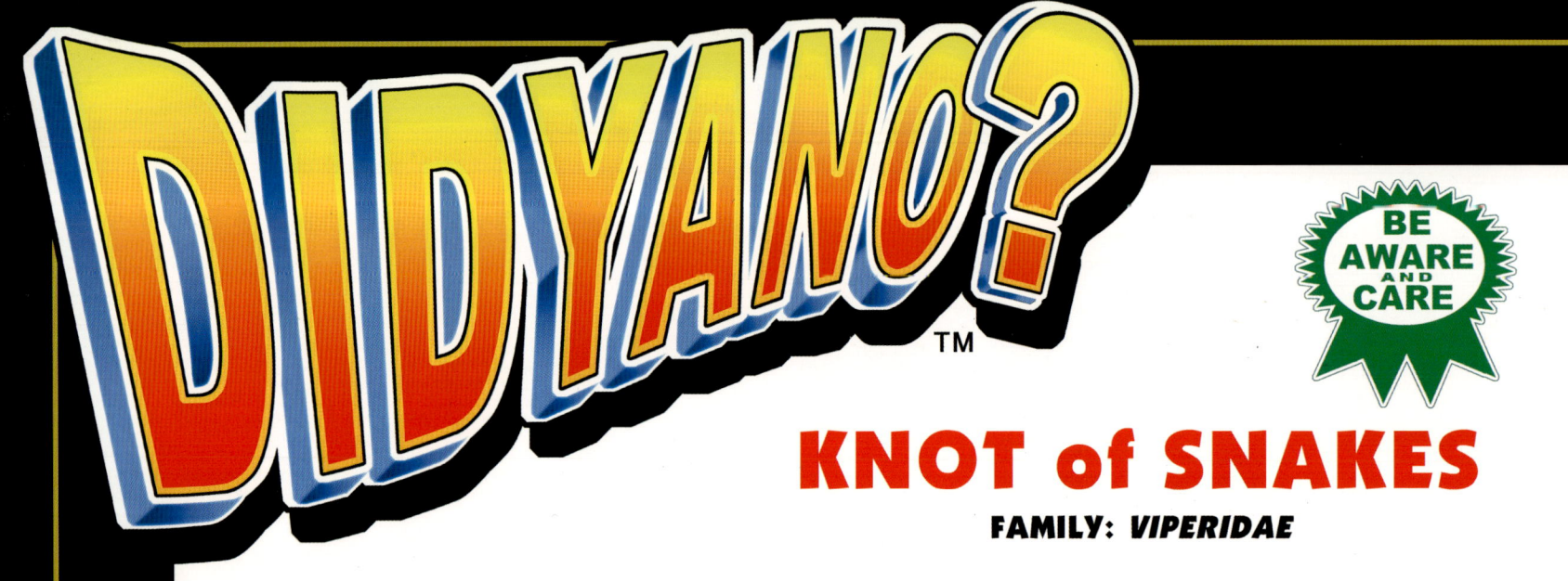

BE AWARE AND CARE

KNOT of SNAKES
FAMILY: *VIPERIDAE*

RATTLESNAKES are poisonous snakes that have rattles on their tails. These hollow rattles make a *buzzing* sound when they are shaken. **Rattlesnakes** continue to grow all their lives, getting bigger and bigger each year. Their scaly skin glistens, but is dry to the touch. The scales vary from yellow to brown to black and there is dark **V** or diamond shaped markings along their backs. The biggest **Rattlesnake** is the *Eastern Diamondback Rattlesnake*.

***Did you know* Rattlesnakes** will lie together in a *knot*? In colder areas, these normally solitary snakes spend the winter in caves or holes with many other **Rattlesnakes**. These snakes look to be all tied together in a *knot*. Very few people are actually bitten by **Rattlesnakes**, yet because their bites are extremely painful and can be fatal, you should always keep alert and watch where you are stepping or putting your hands when you are in the woods.

The *Latin* word for **Rattlesnake** is *Sistrurus* meaning *tail rattler*.

The male **Rattlesnake** is simply called a *Male* and can grow 6 feet long or more and weigh 5-12 pounds. A **Rattlesnake** can only strike a distance that is equal to half its own body length.

The female **Rattlesnake** is simply called a *Female* and gives birth to about 10-12 live young that are born without rattles.

A baby **Rattlesnake** is called a *Snakelet*, *Hatchling* or *Neonate*. A baby **Rattlesnake** is born in the spring and has a full supply of poison or *venom* at birth. It has no rattles until after it sheds its skin, or *molts*, for the first time.

Other family group names are: **Bed**, **Den**, **Pit**, **Nest**, or **Slither**.

Mean as a Rattler describes a person who is very offensive, selfish, or nasty. To be *crooked as a rattler in a cactus patch* is to be extremely dishonest. My Mom always sent me to a room to find something and I rarely ever found it where she said it would be, but it would be close. She would come into the room and see it and always say, *"If it had been a snake, it would have bitten you."*

The sound a **Snake** makes is called a *Hiss*, or in the **Rattlesnake's** case, a *Buzz* or *Rattle*.

Be Aware & Care
Although Eastern Diamondback Rattlesnakes are rapidly disappearing, they are afforded no formal protection. You can show you care and help protect the Rattlesnakes by making others aware that suburban housing and agricultural development destroy vast areas of the Rattlesnakes' habitat. Explain to your family and friends that the Rattlesnakes' role as predator keeps small animal populations, especially rodents, in check.

DIDYANO? Rattlesnakes dance the Rhumba before they mate?

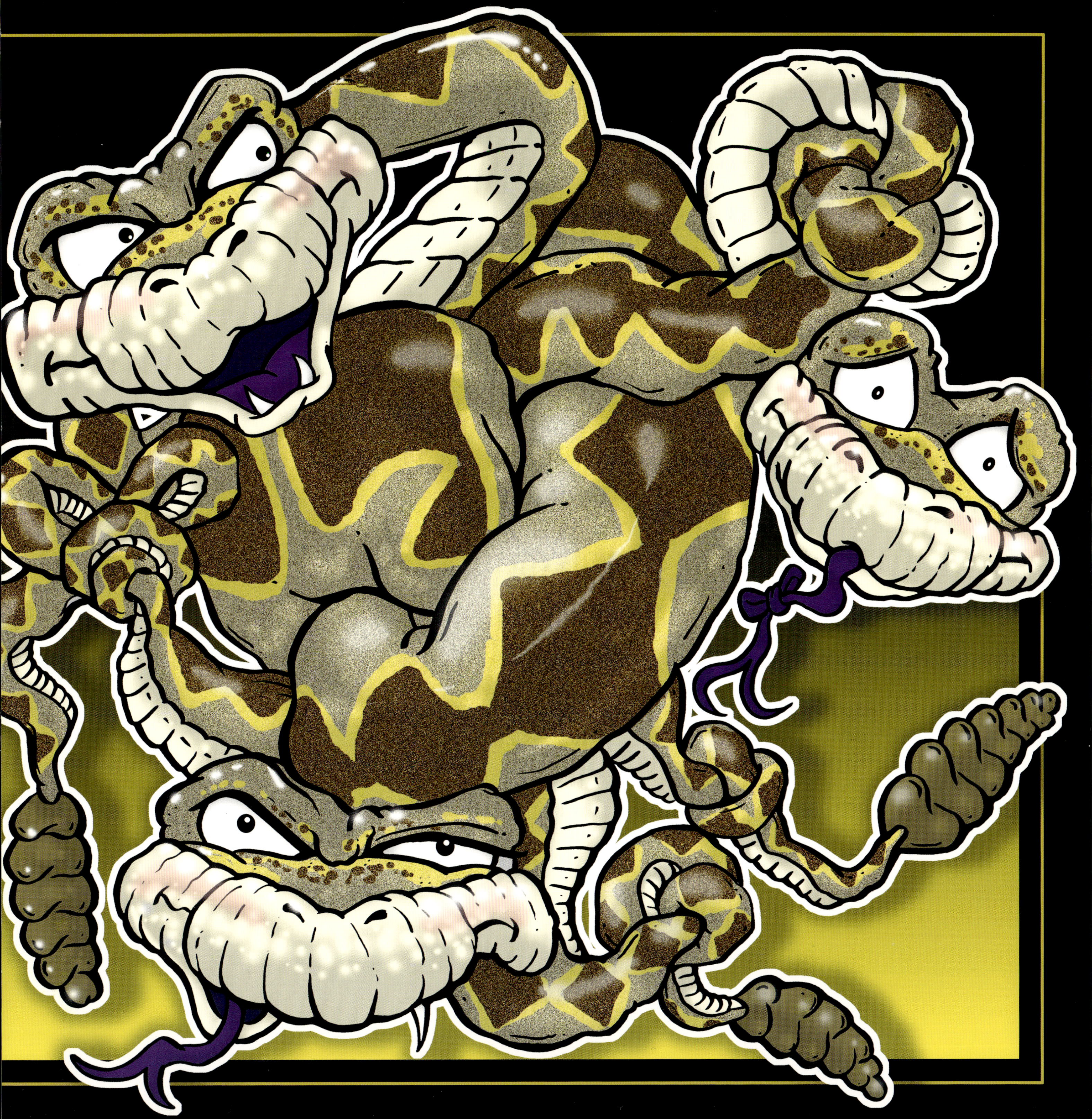

DIDYANO?

BE AWARE AND CARE

PARTY of PEAFOWL
FAMILY: *PHASIANIDAE*

PEAFOWL or *Indian Peafowl* are large, colorful birds, typically blue and green. They are known for their large, colorful tails. These feathers near their tails, or *coverts*, spread out in beautiful *trains* that are more than half of their total body length. Each *covert* boasts a colorful *eye* marking of blue, gold, red, and other colors. Their *trains* can be arched into magnificent fans that reach across the birds' backs and touch the ground on either side.

Did you know that **Peafowl** are forest birds that *roost* in trees at night and gather in a group called a *party*? When you and your family go to a restaurant to eat, the hostess will ask how many are in your group or *party*. Suitable male **Peafowl** may gather several females together in his *party* sometimes called a *harem.* Each female can lay three to five eggs in each of their nests. **Peafowl** make their nests on the ground out of leaves and dirt.

The *Swahili* word for **Peacock** is *Tausi*.

The male **Peafowl** is called a *Peacock* and weighs about 13 pounds. He can grow to the length of 9 feet including his *train*, making him one of the largest flying birds in the world.

The female **Peafowl** is called a *Peahen*. She is not as colorful as the male and her feathers or *plumage* coloring is a mixture of dull green, brown, and gray. The *Peahen* lays decoy eggs in dummy nests far away from the main nest to distract *predators*.

A baby **Peafowl** is called a *Peachick* and resembles a baby turkey or *poult*. The *Peachick* is yellow and brown until it becomes an adult.

Other family group names are: **Pulchritude**, **Ostentation**, **Muster**, or **Pride**.

The sound a **Peafowl** makes is called a *Ca-Caw*.

If you have ever done something you were really proud of then you could be as *proud as a Peacock. The early bird catches the worm* means not to put things off till later, but to do it soon. It's good advice, *unless maybe you're the worm*.

Be Aware & Care
Peafowl were a status symbol through Roman times and the Middle Ages, ensuring their establishment and survival throughout Europe and North America. Fortunately, such a long and close association with humans has given Peafowl an excellent chance of survival. You can show you care and help protect the Peafowl by making others aware why it is important to protect these beautiful birds.

The long feathers of a Peacock are not tail feathers?

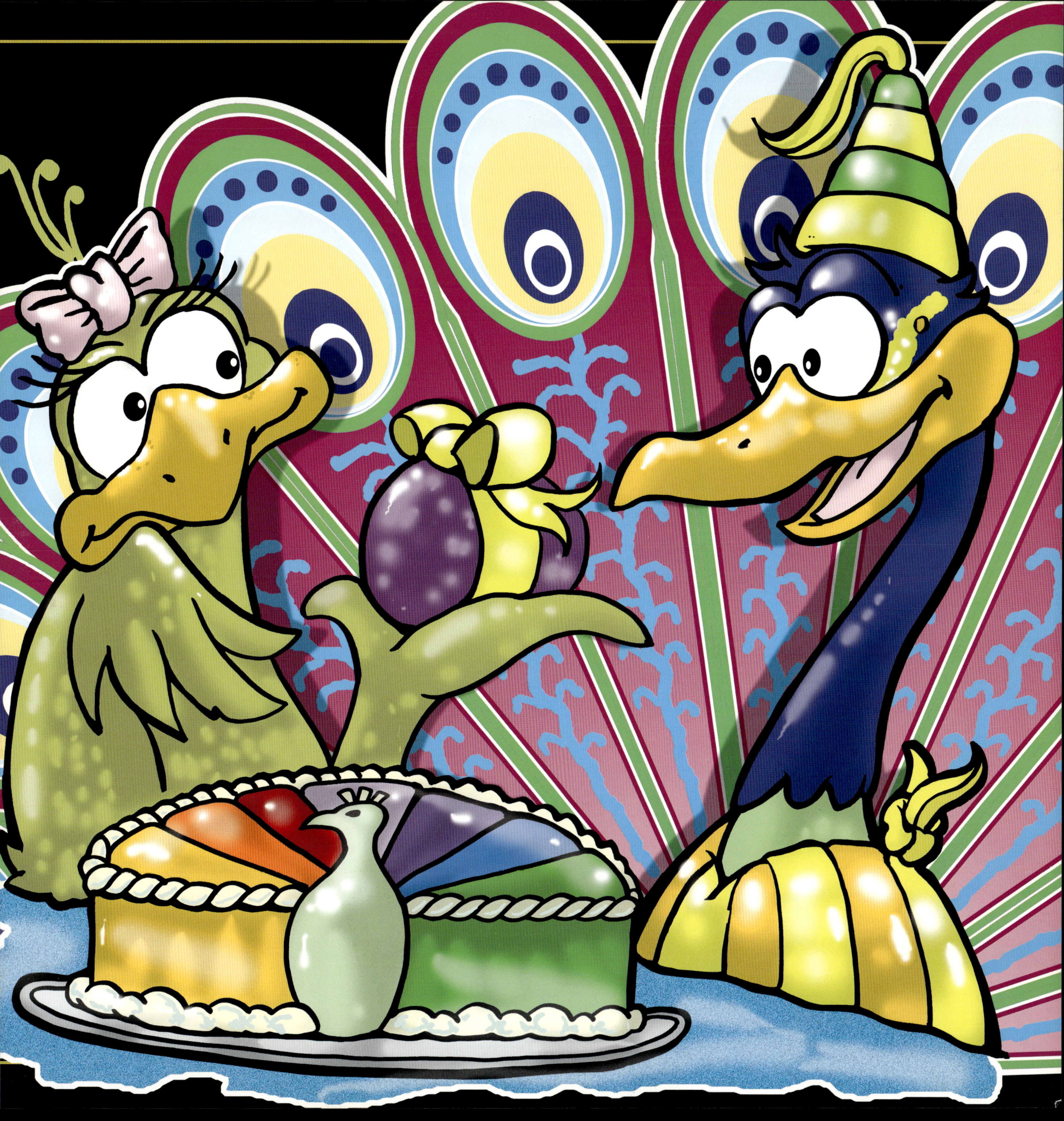

DIDYANO?™

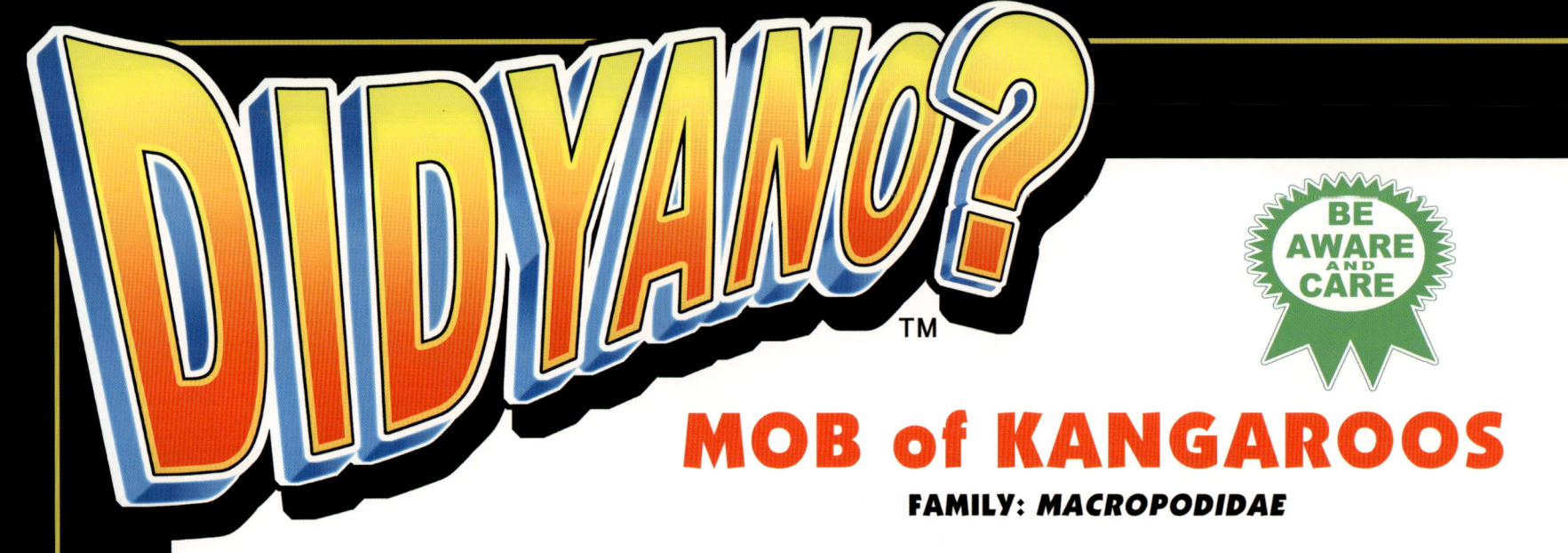

BE AWARE AND CARE

MOB of KANGAROOS
FAMILY: *MACROPODIDAE*

KANGAROOS live in Australia. They have long, powerful hind legs and feet and a long tail. The scientific name, **Macropodidae** means *big-footed*. The hind legs enable the **Kangaroos** to make their amazing leaps of up to 40 feet. On land **Kangaroos** can't move their hind legs independently, only together. But when they are swimming they kick each leg independently. Their heads are small and rabbit-like and their ears are very large. **Kangaroo** fur is soft and woolly.

Did you know **Kangaroos** gather in a group called a *mob*? A *mob* is a large gathering of like things. A **Kangaroo mob** will usually have about 10 or more males and 20 or more females with their young. **Kangaroos** are plant eaters, roaming from place to place, eating a range of grasses and shrubs. Some **Kangaroos** are active in the early morning and late afternoon, but most are *nocturnal* or active at night.

The **Kangaroo** is the **National Symbol for Australia**.

The *Aboriginal* word for **Kangaroo** is *Maloo*.

The male **Red Kangaroo** is called a *Boomer*, *Buck*, or *Jack* and stands nearly 6 feet tall, weighing 200 pounds or more.

The female **Red Kangaroo** is called a *Doe*, *Flyer*, *Jill*, or *Roo* and has one baby each year. The **Red Kangaroo** is the largest living *marsupial* which means she has a *pouch* on her belly where she carries her baby. Her *pouch* is also where her young live, drink milk and develop until it is big enough to live and take care of itself.

A baby **Red Kangaroo** is called a *Joey*. It will live in its mother's *pouch* for 8 months. At birth, a *Joey* cannot see or hear and it does not have fur or back legs.

Other family group names are: **Troop** or **Herd**.

The sound a **Kangaroo** makes is called a *Thump*.

A self-appointed group that decides what to do to someone who is supposed to have done wrong is called a *Kangaroo Court*. *Hop to it* means to get right to it. So, do your school work and ... ***hop to it***!

Be Aware & Care
Human settlement has drastically changed Kangaroo numbers and distribution. You can show you care and help protect the Kangaroos by making others aware why it is important to protect grassland areas for the Kangaroos.

Kangaroos cannot walk backwards?

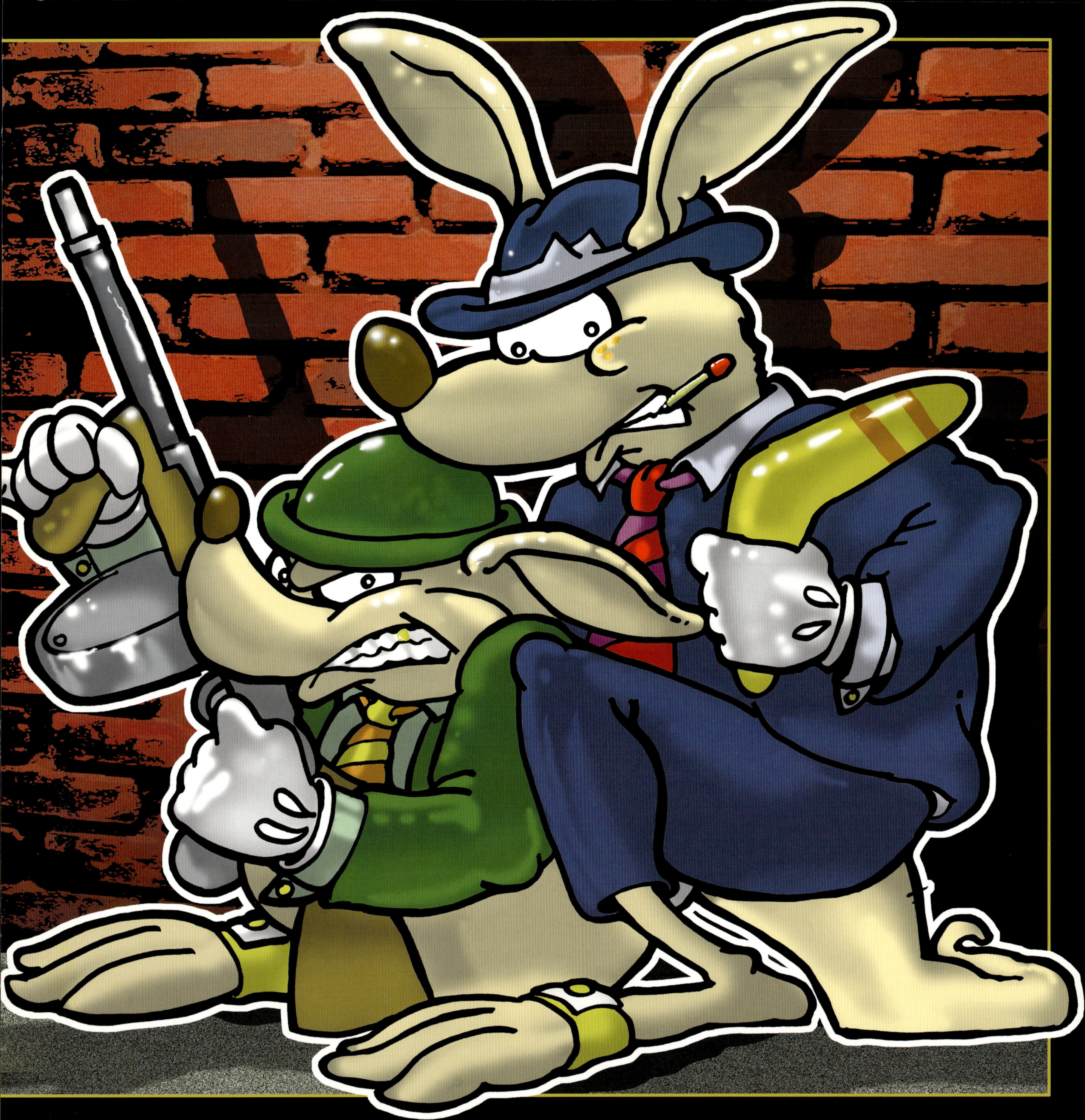

DIDYANO?

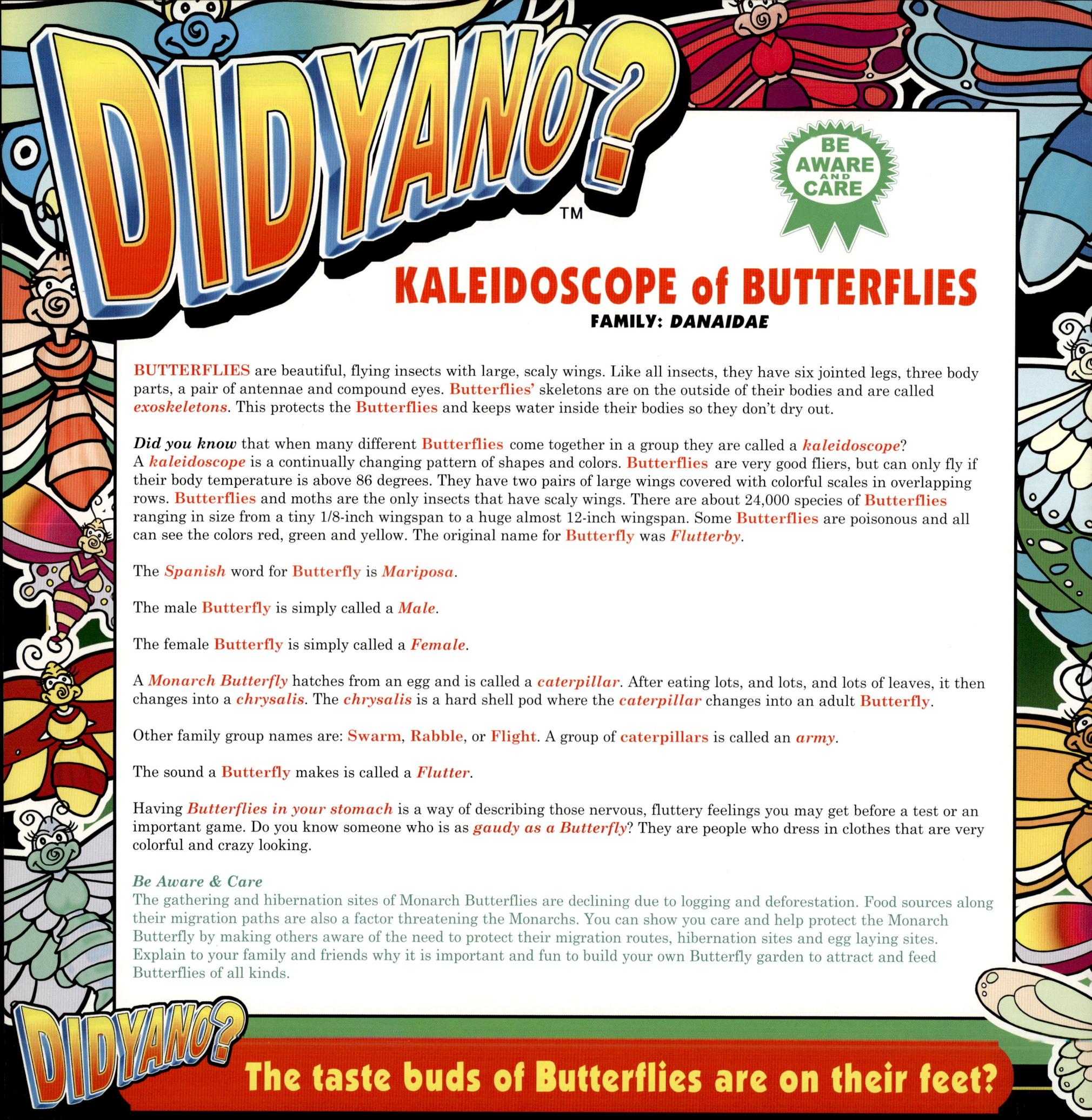

KALEIDOSCOPE of BUTTERFLIES
FAMILY: *DANAIDAE*

BE AWARE AND CARE

BUTTERFLIES are beautiful, flying insects with large, scaly wings. Like all insects, they have six jointed legs, three body parts, a pair of antennae and compound eyes. Butterflies' skeletons are on the outside of their bodies and are called *exoskeletons*. This protects the Butterflies and keeps water inside their bodies so they don't dry out.

Did you know that when many different Butterflies come together in a group they are called a *kaleidoscope*? A *kaleidoscope* is a continually changing pattern of shapes and colors. Butterflies are very good fliers, but can only fly if their body temperature is above 86 degrees. They have two pairs of large wings covered with colorful scales in overlapping rows. Butterflies and moths are the only insects that have scaly wings. There are about 24,000 species of Butterflies ranging in size from a tiny 1/8-inch wingspan to a huge almost 12-inch wingspan. Some Butterflies are poisonous and all can see the colors red, green and yellow. The original name for Butterfly was *Flutterby*.

The *Spanish* word for Butterfly is *Mariposa*.

The male Butterfly is simply called a *Male*.

The female Butterfly is simply called a *Female*.

A *Monarch Butterfly* hatches from an egg and is called a *caterpillar*. After eating lots, and lots, and lots of leaves, it then changes into a *chrysalis*. The *chrysalis* is a hard shell pod where the *caterpillar* changes into an adult Butterfly.

Other family group names are: Swarm, Rabble, or Flight. A group of caterpillars is called an *army*.

The sound a Butterfly makes is called a *Flutter*.

Having Butterflies in your stomach is a way of describing those nervous, fluttery feelings you may get before a test or an important game. Do you know someone who is as *gaudy as a Butterfly*? They are people who dress in clothes that are very colorful and crazy looking.

Be Aware & Care
The gathering and hibernation sites of Monarch Butterflies are declining due to logging and deforestation. Food sources along their migration paths are also a factor threatening the Monarchs. You can show you care and help protect the Monarch Butterfly by making others aware of the need to protect their migration routes, hibernation sites and egg laying sites. Explain to your family and friends why it is important and fun to build your own Butterfly garden to attract and feed Butterflies of all kinds.

The taste buds of Butterflies are on their feet?

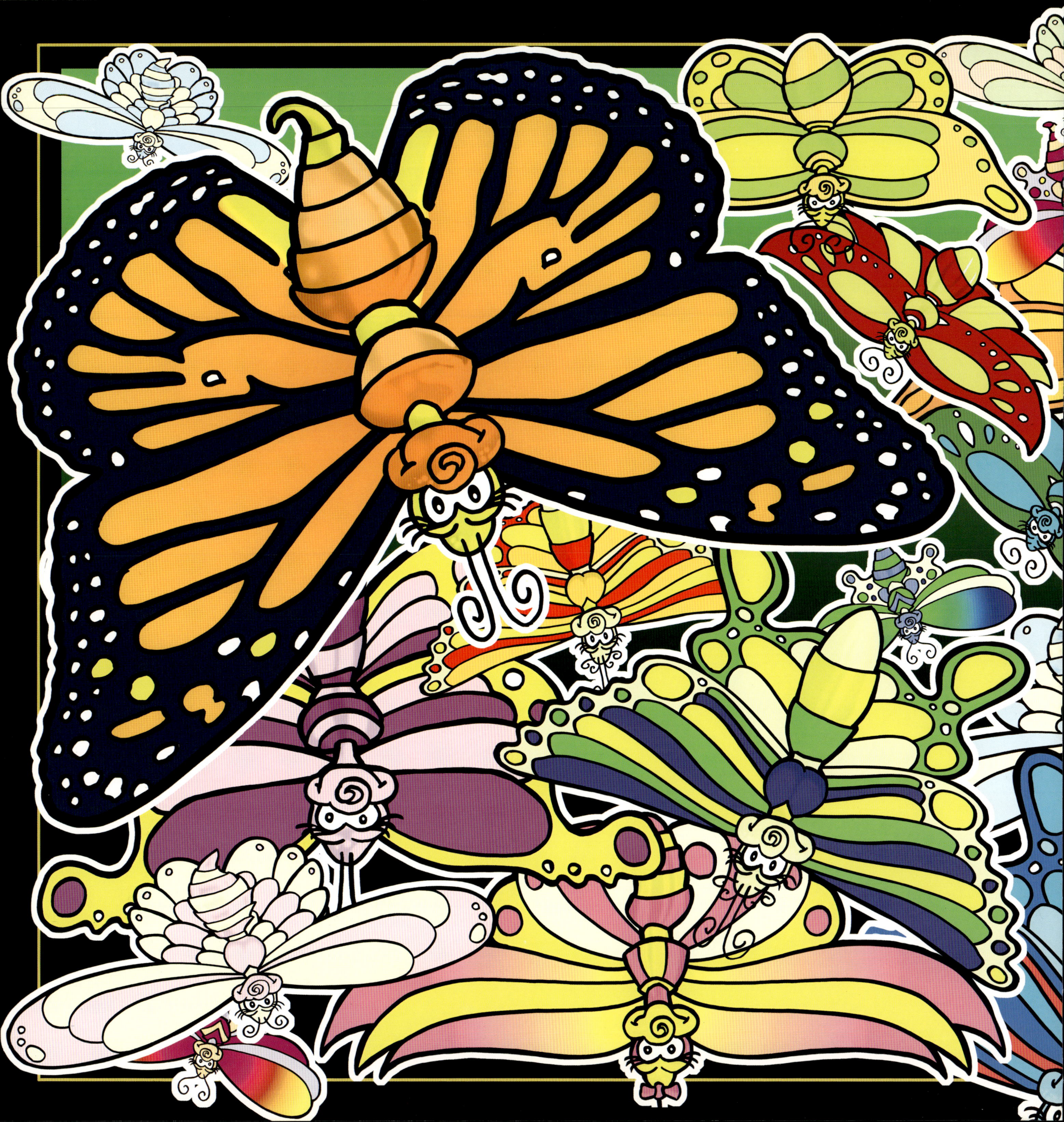

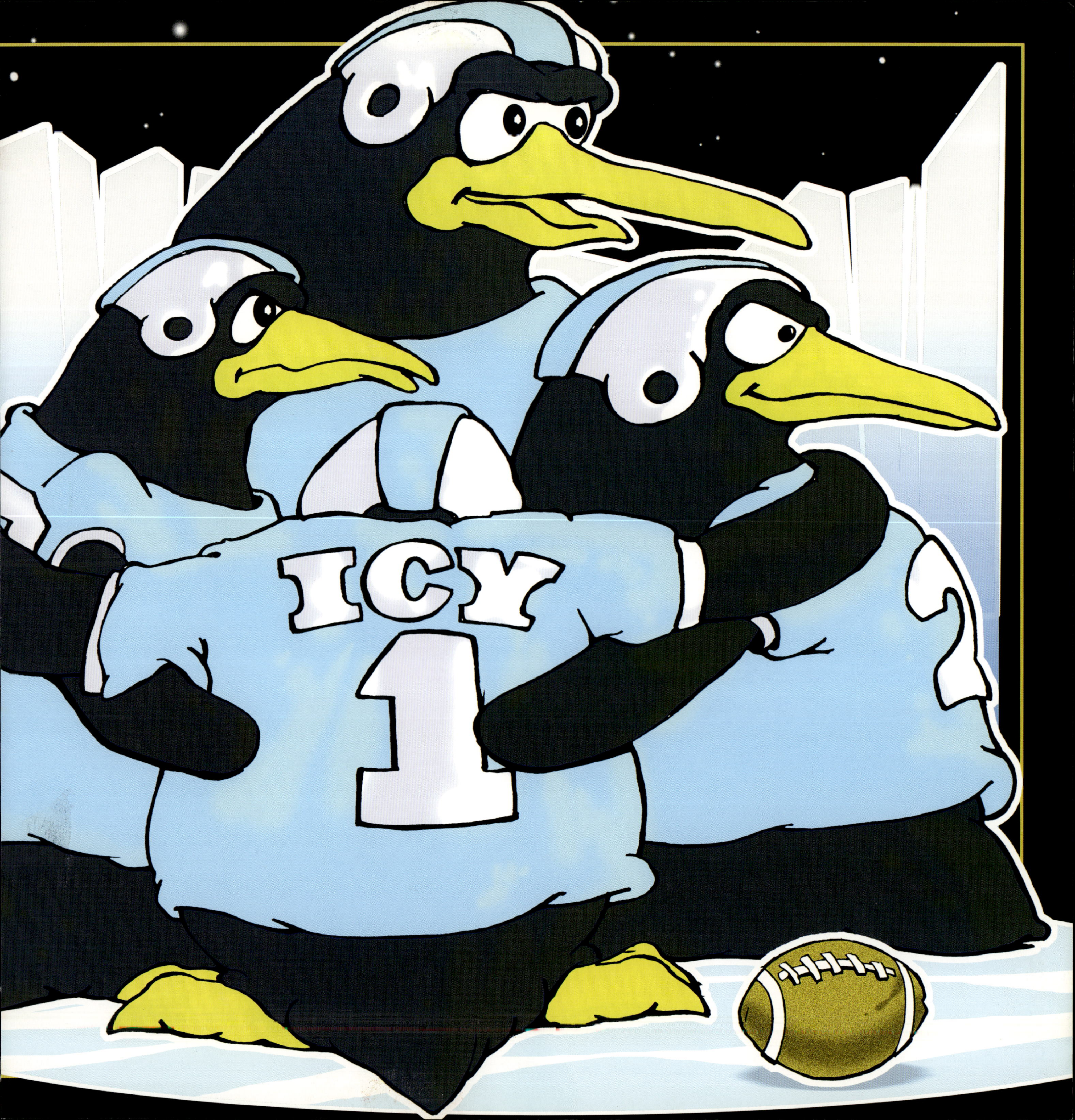
ICY
1

DIDYANO?

BE AWARE AND CARE

HUDDLE of PENGUINS
FAMILY: *SPHENISIDAE*

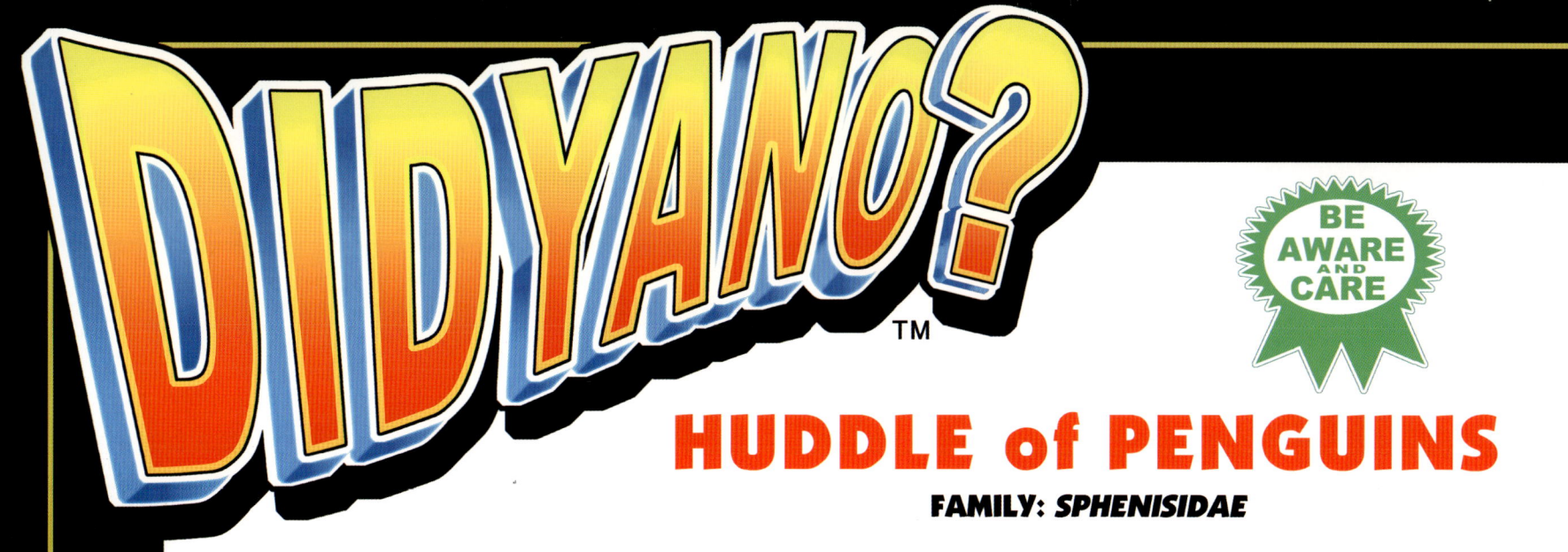

PENGUINS are birds that can't fly; *they swim!* **Emperor Penguins** are the largest of all **Penguins**, easily recognized by their black cap, blue-grey neck, orange ear-patches and bills, and yellow breasts. There is a thick layer of fat or *blubber* under their skin that helps keep them warm. **Emperor Penguins** spend most of their lives at sea, using their wings as *flippers*. They march from the sea to their nesting grounds as far as 70 miles inland. **Emperor Penguins** rock backwards on their heels while holding their toes up. They support themselves by their stiff tail feathers that sometimes freeze to the ice! So to be as cold as a **Penguin's** tail, is very, very, very cold!

Did you know **Emperor Penguins** gather in a group called a *huddle*? They *huddle* together to keep warm on the Antarctic ice. The winter nights are long and the period of darkness can last more than 20 hours. The male may spend most of a 24-hour period sleeping to conserve energy. He doesn't get to swim or eat for 60 days. His one and only job is to keep the egg warm and off the icy ground. This is called *incubation*. He does this by keeping the egg on the tops of his feet and under his belly feathers. During this time he can lose up to half of his body weight. After the egg has hatched, the female returns to find the male and her new baby. The male gives the chick over to the female and heads out to sea to feed. Both care for the baby until it is able to enter the water to find food on its own.

The *Spanish* word for **Penguin** is *Pingüino*.

The male **Emperor Penguin** is called a *Male* or *Cock*. He stands 40 inches tall and weighs 85-90 pounds. The male **Penguin** fasts nearly two months through the Antarctic winter, *incubating* the egg.

The female **Emperor Penguin** is called a *Female* or *Hen*. She will mate with only one male during the mating season and will lay only one egg.

A baby **Emperor Penguin** is called a *Chick* or *Fledgling* and is gray in color when it is born.

Other family group names are: **Colony**, **Rookery**, **Parade**, or **Parcel**.

The sound a baby **Emperor Penguin** makes is called a *Bleat*.

Be Aware & Care
Emperor Penguins face a number of threats, including destruction of nesting habitats, competition with fishermen for fish and shrimp, and introduced predators such as rats, dogs and foxes which eat penguin eggs and young. You can show you care and help protect the Emperor Penguins by making others aware that the greatest potential threat to Emperor Penguins is extreme climate change.

DIDYANO?
Emperor Penguins can dive 1,700 ft underwater?

SEA COW XING

DIDYANO?

BE AWARE AND CARE

HERD of MANATEES
FAMILY: *TRICHECIDAE*

MANATEES are gray in color with cigar shaped bodies that taper to a flat, paddle-shaped tail. Their heads and faces are wrinkled and have short whiskers on their snouts. **Manatees** have two front limbs called *flippers* and on each *flipper* are three to four *flipper-nails*. They are surprisingly agile in water and individual **Manatees** have been seen doing rolls, somersaults, and even swimming upside-down.

Did you know that **Manatees** live in a group called a *herd*? The **Manatee** has been called a *Sea Cow* because it is big and grazes on grasses in the water. Like cattle it lives in a *herd*. **Manatees** are often found in rivers, estuaries and in the coastal waters of the Gulf of Mexico and the Atlantic Ocean. During the winter, when the water turns cold, they swim inland to warm waterholes called *springs*. In these areas is where the **Manatees** live and feed. Large adults feast on nearly 45 to 65 pounds of sea grasses and plant leaves daily, keeping waterways clear and open. Many **Manatees** have scars on their backs and tails from being injured by boats. Some **Manatees** do not survive when boats hit them. **Manatees** breathe air so they must rise to the surface often. They may rest submerged at the water's bottom or just below the surface, coming up to breathe on the average of every three to four minutes. However, they have been known to stay submerged for as long as 20 minutes. That is probably why the **Manatees** stay in shallow waters less than 20 feet deep.

The *Spanish* name for **Manatee** is *Manati*. The Maya people had a special process to prepare dried **Manatee** meat, which they called *buccan*. Pirates who preyed upon the ships of Spanish explorers along the Guatemalan coast relied so much upon *buccan* as a staple in their diet that they became known as *buccaneers*.

The male **Manatee** is called a *Bull* and may grow over 10 feet long, and weigh between 800 and 1,200 pounds or more.

The female **Manatee** is called a *Cow* and nurses her young from glands behind her *flippers*.

A baby **Manatee** is called a *Calf* and is 3-4 feet long at birth and can weigh 40-70 pounds. The *Calf* stays with its mother for as long as two years.

Other family group names are: *Family* or *Pod*.

The sound a **Manatee** makes is called *Chirps* and *Squeaks*.

Be Aware & Care
All species of Manatees are protected to some extent by national or local laws in every country they inhabit. The greatest threats to Manatees are loss of habitat and boat collisions. You can show you care and help protect the Manatees by making others aware that federal and state laws have been passed that protect the Manatees. Federal laws prohibit hunting, capturing, killing, or harassing these animals.

DIDYANO? Sailors of old believed that the Manatees were mermaids?

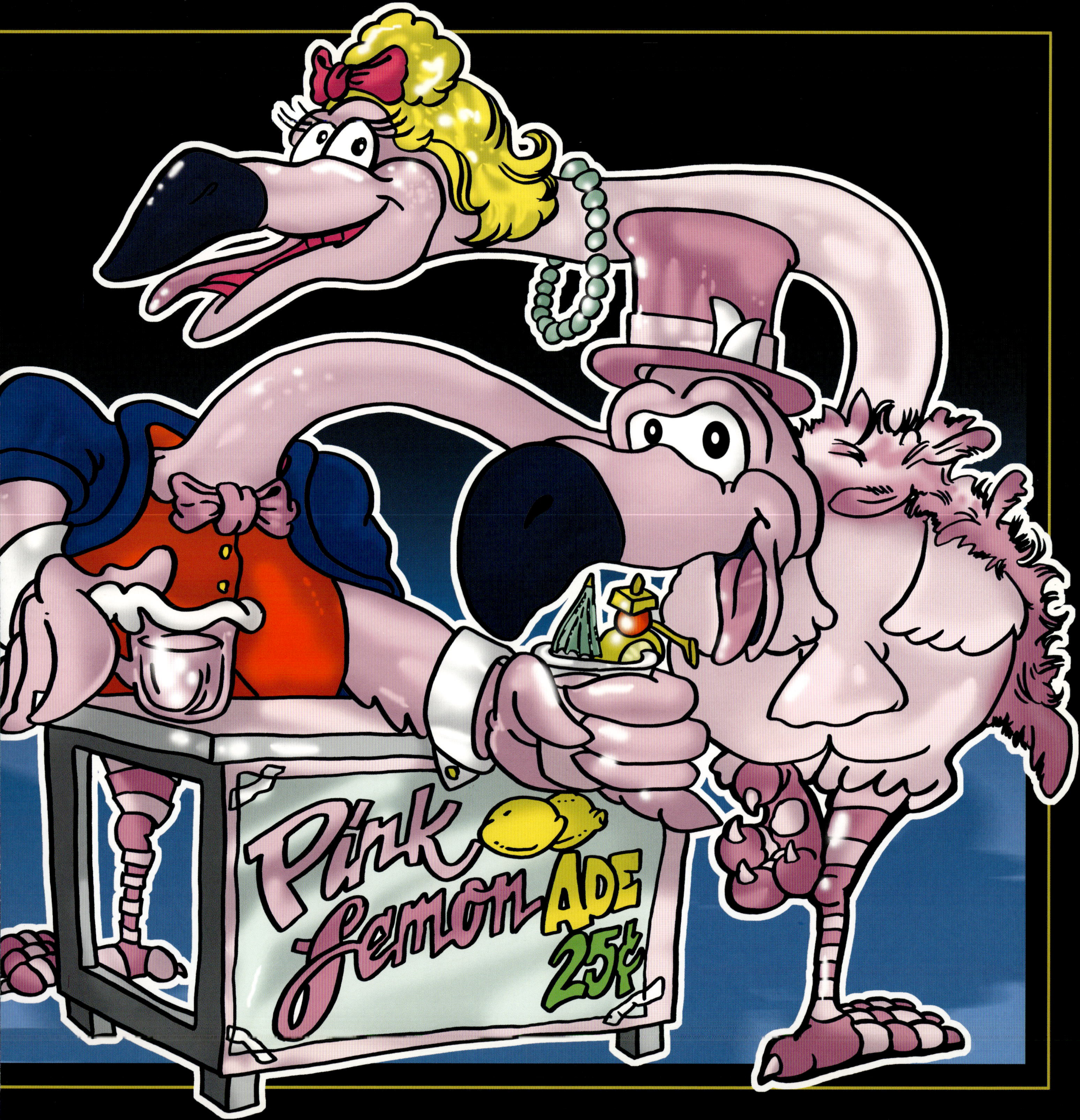
Pink Lemon ADE
25¢

DIDYANO?

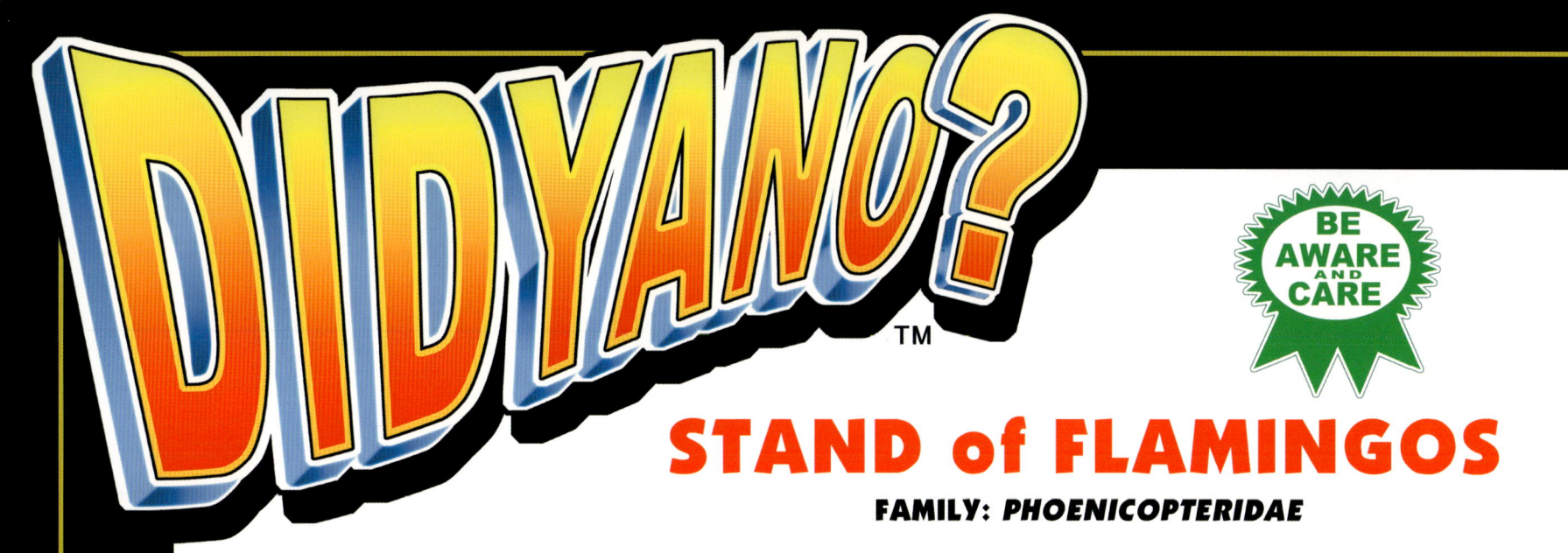

BE AWARE AND CARE

STAND of FLAMINGOS
FAMILY: *PHOENICOPTERIDAE*

FLAMINGOS are tall birds with long legs and necks, but have small heads. The *Pink Flamingos* are really gray in color, but get their bright pink or crimson feathers from the types of food they eat. Their diet is mainly shrimp and *plankton*. Flamingos wade through the shallow water and mud with their heads upside-down sucking in the muck through their bills and squirting it back out over their very large tongues. Flamingos can eat and swallow only when their heads are upside-down. The Flamingo has the largest tongue of any bird. The Ancient Romans ate the Flamingos tongues and considered them a delicacy.

Did you know Flamingos sleep in a group called a *stand*? Flamingos are known to nap with their bills tucked under their wings while *standing* on one leg. They are unique among birds in that both mom and dad provide their babies with a type of milk called *crop milk* that helps fight diseases. This is real milk from a special gland the Flamingos have and not just half digested food the parents spit up from their stomachs like some other birds do.

The *Spanish* word for Flamingo is *Flamenco*. Flamingo is a *Portuguese* word that means *red goose*.

The male Flamingo is called a *Cock*. He stands nearly 5 feet tall and has a 5-foot wing span. He can live to be about 50 years old.

The female Flamingo is called a *Hen*. She and the *Cock* build their nest out of mud. The *Hen* lays only one egg a year.

A baby Flamingo is called a *Chick* or *Hatchling* and is white when it is born.

Other family group names are: Flamboyance

The sound a Flamingo makes is called a *Racket* or *Squawk*.

Just because someone looks alright doesn't mean they are, because *fine feathers do not make fine birds*. One day you will leave home and have children of your own. All children must eventually leave home and we sometimes say that they must *fly or leave the nest*. Moms and Dads then have what is called *the empty nest syndrome*.

Be Aware & Care
The Flamingos uses to man are unfortunately one of their biggest problems. In the past, their tongues were a rare, pickled delicacy, and their plumage was sometimes sought for its vibrant color. You can show you care and help protect the Flamingos by making others aware that habitat destruction is by far the Flamingo's greatest challenge.

DIDYANO? There are more plastic Flamingos in America than real ones?

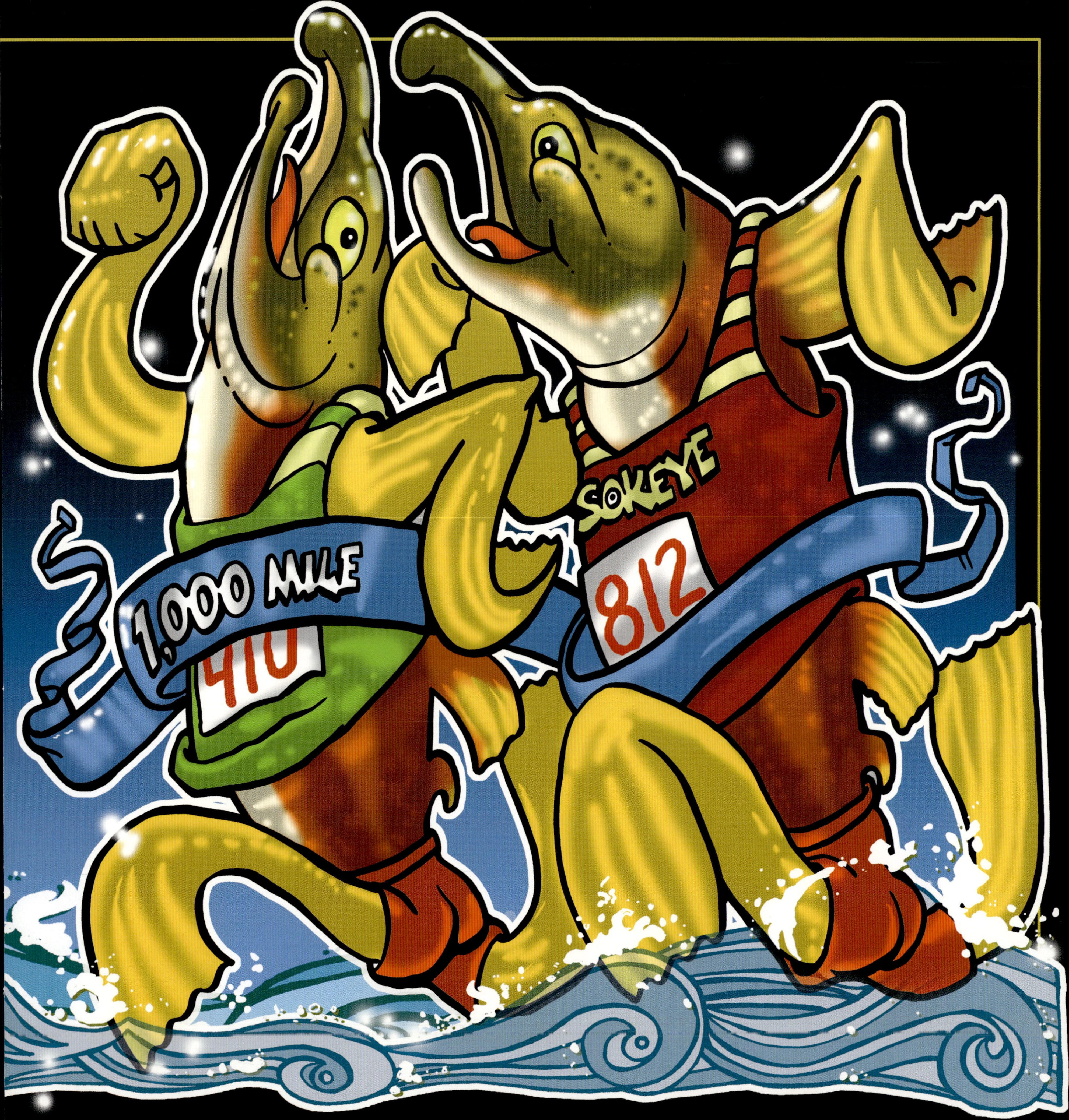
1,000 MILE
410
SOKEYE
812

DIDYANO?

BE AWARE AND CARE

RUN of SALMON
FAMILY: *SALMONIDAE*

SALMON live in the Atlantic and Pacific Oceans as well as the Great Lakes and other landlocked lakes. Salmon have red or silvery skin with spots on their backs and fins. They eat other little fish, squid, insects, and they really like shrimp. Many people eat Salmon and the meat of some is red and pink in color. The *King Salmon* is the title given to the *Chinook* because it is the largest species of Salmon in the world.

Did you know many types of Salmon migrate in a group called a *run*? Of course Salmon do not have legs to *run*. Going from one place to another and achieving a specific goal is called a *run*. Some Salmon are born in fresh water, migrate to the ocean and return to fresh water to lay their eggs and *spawn*. While heading upstream, Salmon swim up waterfalls and over large rocks and logs. Some Salmon become lunch for bears, eagles and wolves, but all will die after *spawning*. Many people believe that Salmon return to the exact spot where they were born.

The *Spanish* word for Salmon is *Salmon*.

The male Salmon is called a *Kipper* or *Jack*. The biggest Salmon is the *Chinook*, which can weigh up to 120 pounds.

The female Salmon is called a *Bagget*, *Hen* or *Raun*. Using her tail, she will dig a nest in the rocks and gravel called a *redd* and lay nearly 5,000 eggs.

A baby Salmon is called a *Samlet*, *Skegger* or *Smolt*. The eggs will hatch into *alevin* or *sac fry* and quickly develop into *parr*. The *parr* stay for one to three years in the fresh water streams before becoming *smolt*.

Other family group names are: Bind, Gib, School, or Shoal.

The sound a Salmon makes is called a *Splash*. Salmon themselves don't make sounds, but as they swim up rivers and jump, *splashes* are what can be heard.

The phrase, *you're going the right way only backwards*, usually means you are confused about the facts, but may end with the right decision anyway. *Smelt* always swim with their face into the water's current, so to get to the ocean, they swim facing forward while the current pushes them backwards to the sea. *Sounds a little fishy to me!*

Be Aware & Care
Salmon are sensitive to environmental changes and are dependent upon both fresh and saltwater habitats. You can show you care and help protect the Salmon by making others aware why it is important to protect the Salmon and their spawning grounds from pollution and habitat destruction. You might also make them aware of the dangers of over fishing. Many species of animals rely on the runs of Salmon as a food source.

DIDYANO? Some Salmon may travel 1,000 mls upstream to spawn?

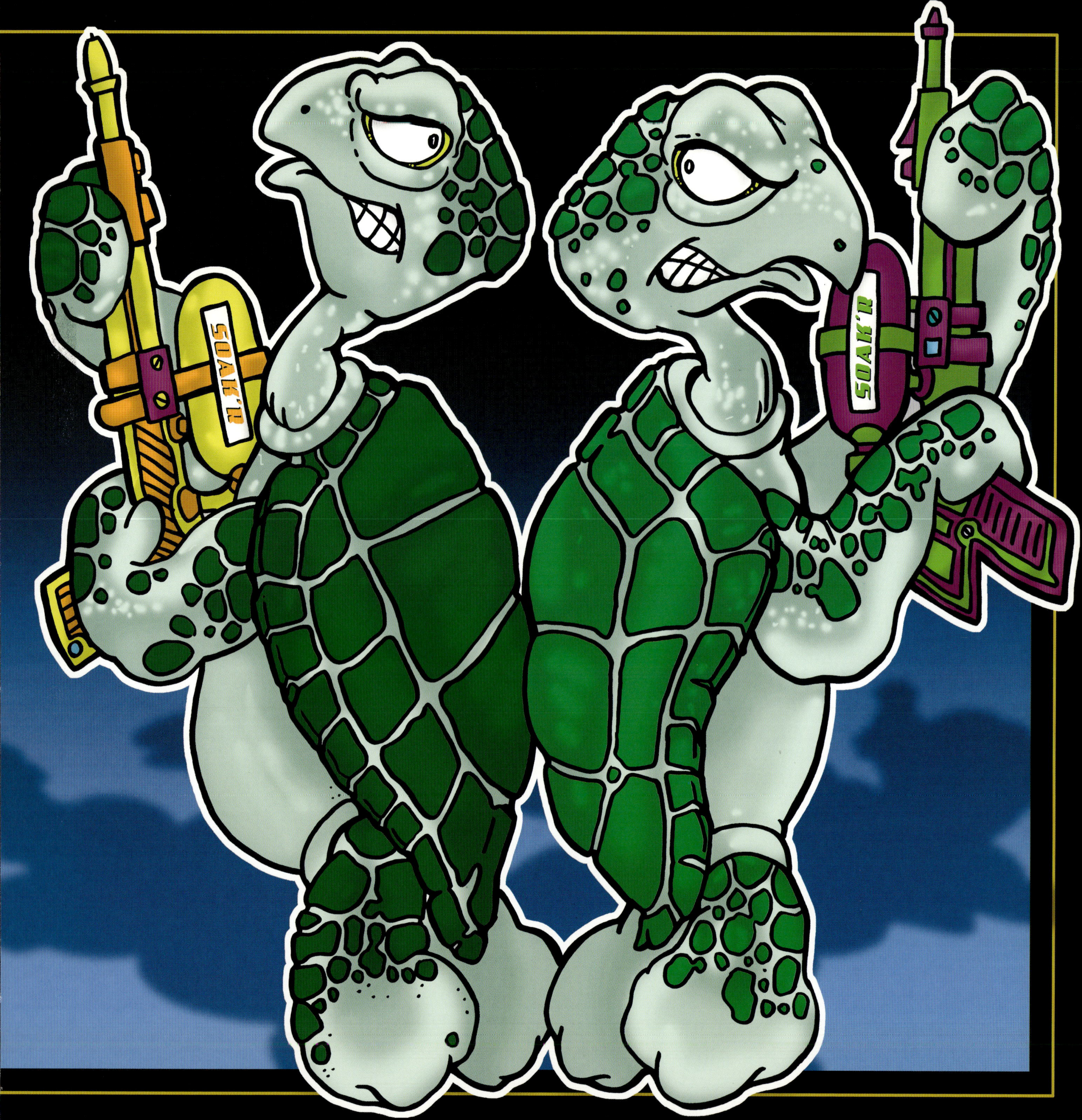
SOAK'R
SOAK'R

DIDYANO?™

BE AWARE AND CARE

DULE of SEA TURTLES
FAMILY: *CHELONIDAE*

SEA TURTLES are turtles that live nearly all their lives in the warm waters of the oceans. Unlike land turtles, **Sea Turtles** do not have legs for walking; they have *flippers*. Their heads, tails, and legs remain out of their shells at all times unlike land turtles that can pull them completely into their shells for protection. **Sea Turtles** are unique in that they are one of the few creatures to have two skeletons; an internal one and their shell. There are seven living kinds of **Sea Turtles**: *Flatback*, *Green*, *Hawksbill*, *Kemp's Ridley*, *Leatherback*, *Loggerhead*, and *Olive Ridley*.

Did you know newly hatched **Sea Turtles** travel in a group called a *dule*? A *dule* or *dole* is a small amount of something that is set free, turned loose, or handed out. Adult **Sea Turtles** live alone except during mating. Baby **Sea Turtles** hatch from a *clutch* of eggs buried beneath the sand and the babies crawl free from their nests to the sea as a group.

The *Spanish* word for **Sea Turtle** is *Tortuga*. The *Spanish* word *Arribada* means *arrival* and is used to refer to the annual arrival of nesting **Olive Ridley Sea Turtles** to beaches in Mexico.

The male **Sea Turtle** is simply called a *Male*. The male **Leatherback Turtle** is the largest living turtle in the world. He can weigh as much as 1,600 pounds and can dive to 3,000 feet below the ocean's surface.

The female **Sea Turtle** is simply called a *Female*. Depending on the species, the female will mature around 15-20 years of age. She will return to the very same beach to lay her eggs, where she herself hatched. She may lay as many as 100 eggs per nest and dig 3-4 nests during the hatching season.

A baby **Sea Turtle** is called a *Hatchling* and is born in a nest under the sand. A *Hatchling* is only about 2 inches long at birth. A **Sea Turtle** can swim 10-20 miles per hour once it becomes an adult and may live to be over 100 years old.

Other family group names are: **Bevy**, **Nest**, **Bale**, **Dole**, or **Turn**.

The sound a **Sea Turtle** makes is called a *Grunt*.

Be Aware & Care
The greatest threat to Sea Turtles has been man hunting them for their meat and shells. Other threats include egg poaching, habitat destruction, pollution, and boat strikes. You can show you care and help protect Sea Turtles by making others aware why it is important to protect their nesting grounds and keep the waters where Sea Turtles live free of trash and pollution. Make sure you properly dispose of things that Sea Turtles can swallow or get tangled in. These include ribbons, balloons, plastic bags, fishing line and fishing nets. If you live in an area where Sea Turtles are found, volunteer to help with rehabilitation and conservation work.

DIDYANO?

Sea Turtles cry large tears that rid their bodies of excess salt?

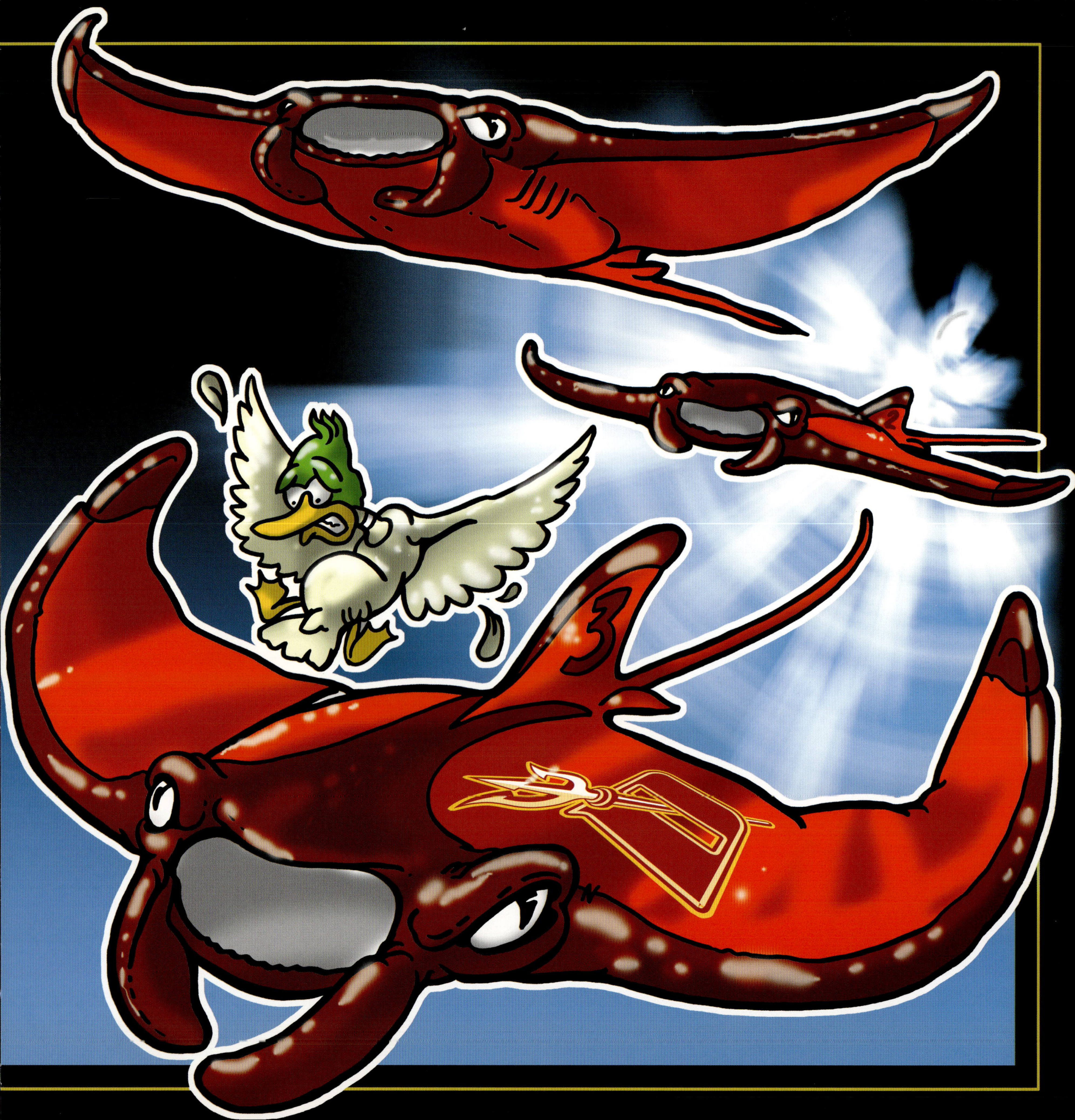

DIDYANO?

FLIGHT of MANTA RAYS
FAMILY: *MOBULIDAE*

BE AWARE AND CARE

MANTA RAYS are large, bat shaped fish that swim in warm, tropical, ocean waters. Manta Rays have dark black-blue backs and white undersides. The Giant Manta Ray is the largest of the rays. Like sharks, they have five gills, but their gills are located on the underside of their bodies. Manta Rays are harmless, majestic creatures with short, whip shaped tails. Unlike many rays, Manta Rays do not have sharp barbs or stinging spines on their tails. They have unique horns on either side of their head called *cephalic lobes* that directs food called *plankton* into their mouths. These horns and their eerie behavior of circling small fishing boats at sea are what earned the Manta Ray the nickname of *Devilfish* or *Devil Ray*.

Did you know Manta Rays gather in groups called a *flight*? They have distinctive wings or *pectoral fins* that can measure over 20 feet from tip to tip. Manta Rays use their wing shaped fins to glide or *fly* through the water. They are very acrobatic and are known to leap high out of the water.

The *Spanish* word Manta means *cloak* or *blanket*. When swimming close to the ocean's surface, the Manta Ray resembles a large cape or blanket that has been spread-out on the water.

The male Manta Ray is called a *Devil*. He and the female are solitary, free swimmers. He is not a territorial animal and has been known to *migrate* or swim very far in search of *plankton* rich waters.

The female Manta Ray is called a *She-Devil*. She will carry 1 or 2 eggs inside her body until they hatch. She will then give birth to her young which are rolled up like tubes.

A baby Manta Ray is called a *Manta Pup*. The *She-Devil* releases the *Manta Pup* into the water. It will become active and start to swim as soon as it unrolls. The newborn of the Giant Manta Ray is fairly large, weighing 20-30 pounds. Its fins can span 4 feet and the *Manta Pup* can generally protect itself from predators.

Other family group names are: School or Rendezvous.

The sound a Manta Ray makes is a *Flop*. When it leaps into the air it generally *belly-flops* back into the water.

Be Aware & Care
In many parts of the world, some Manta Rays are commercially important food sources. Currently, Manta Rays are not considered threatened or endangered. You can show you care and help protect the Manta Rays by making others aware that due to man's impact on the marine environment, concern is mounting for the future of the Manta Rays.

The Manta Ray has the largest brain of any fish?

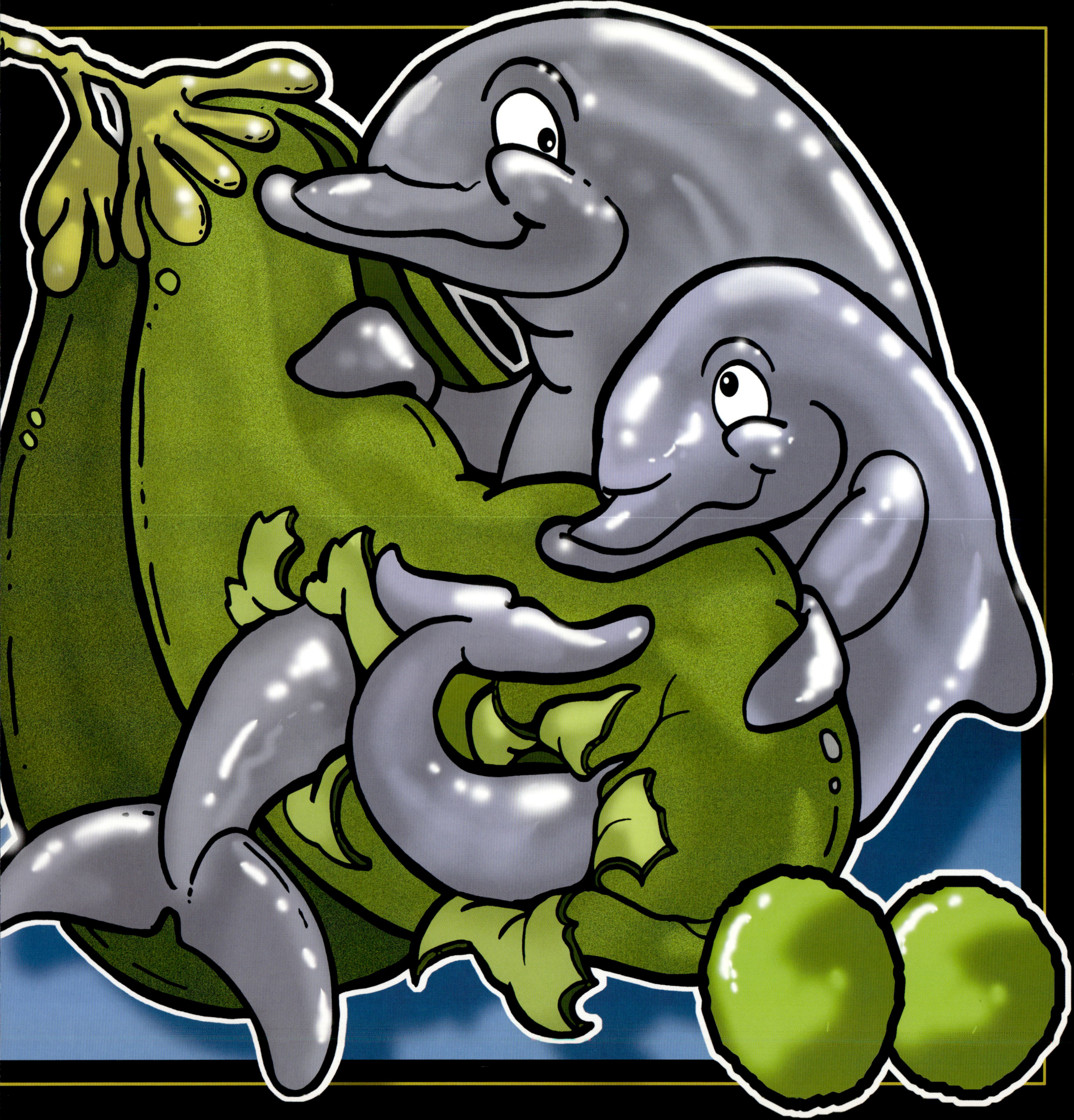

DIDYANO?

BE AWARE AND CARE

POD of DOLPHINS
FAMILY: *DELPHINIDAE*

DOLPHINS are mammals, not fish. They are generally gray and have a distinct beak for a mouth. The **Dolphins'** teeth are shaped like ice-cream cones. They are warm-blooded like humans and give birth to one baby at a time. **Dolphins** are powerful swimmers found all over the world and in all seas. Like a bat, **Dolphins** use high-pitched sounds or *echolocation* to navigate and hunt. Fish and squid are the diet of most **Dolphins**. They have been seen hunting and working together to herd fish into tight schools or balls.

Did you know **Dolphins** travel together in a group called a *pod*? They travel in *pods* and are often seen very close to shore. **Dolphins** can travel in groups of hundreds when offshore and can merge with other *pods* to form *superpods*.

The **Dolphin's** brain is divided into two sections called *lobes*. It is believed that a **Dolphin** never sleeps. When one side of its brain shuts down, the other side stays awake and alert. Each of the **Dolphin's** eyes is connected to a different side of the brain. Because of this, a **Dolphin** can still see when it is sleeping, making it difficult for predators to sneak up on it.

The *Spanish* word for **Dolphin** is *Delfin*.

The male **Bottlenose Dolphin** is called a *Bull*. He will grow to become about 12 feet in length, weigh over 500 pounds and live up to 40 years.

The female **Bottlenose Dolphin** is called a *Cow*. She is pregnant for 1 year and has only one baby at a time. Sometimes another female helps the mother **Dolphin** with her new baby. This helpful **Dolphin** is called a *midwife* or an *auntie*.

A baby **Bottlenose Dolphin** is called a *Calf*. At birth the *Calf* will be 3 feet long. It will live side-by-side with its mother for up to 2 years.

Other family group names are: **Team**, **School**, or **Herd**.

The sounds a **Dolphin** makes are called *Clicks* and *Whistles*.

The phrase *smile like a Dolphin* refers to someone with a very big grin on his face.

Be Aware & Care
It is harmful and illegal to feed or harass wild Dolphins. Dolphins, like all marine mammals, are protected by the U.S. Marine Mammal Protection Act (MMPA) of 1972. You can show you care and help protect the Dolphins by making others aware why it is important to protect the Dolphins and the waters in which they live, eat and breed. In 2007 it was announced that the Yangtze river-dolphin of China was now extinct.

Dolphins have belly buttons?

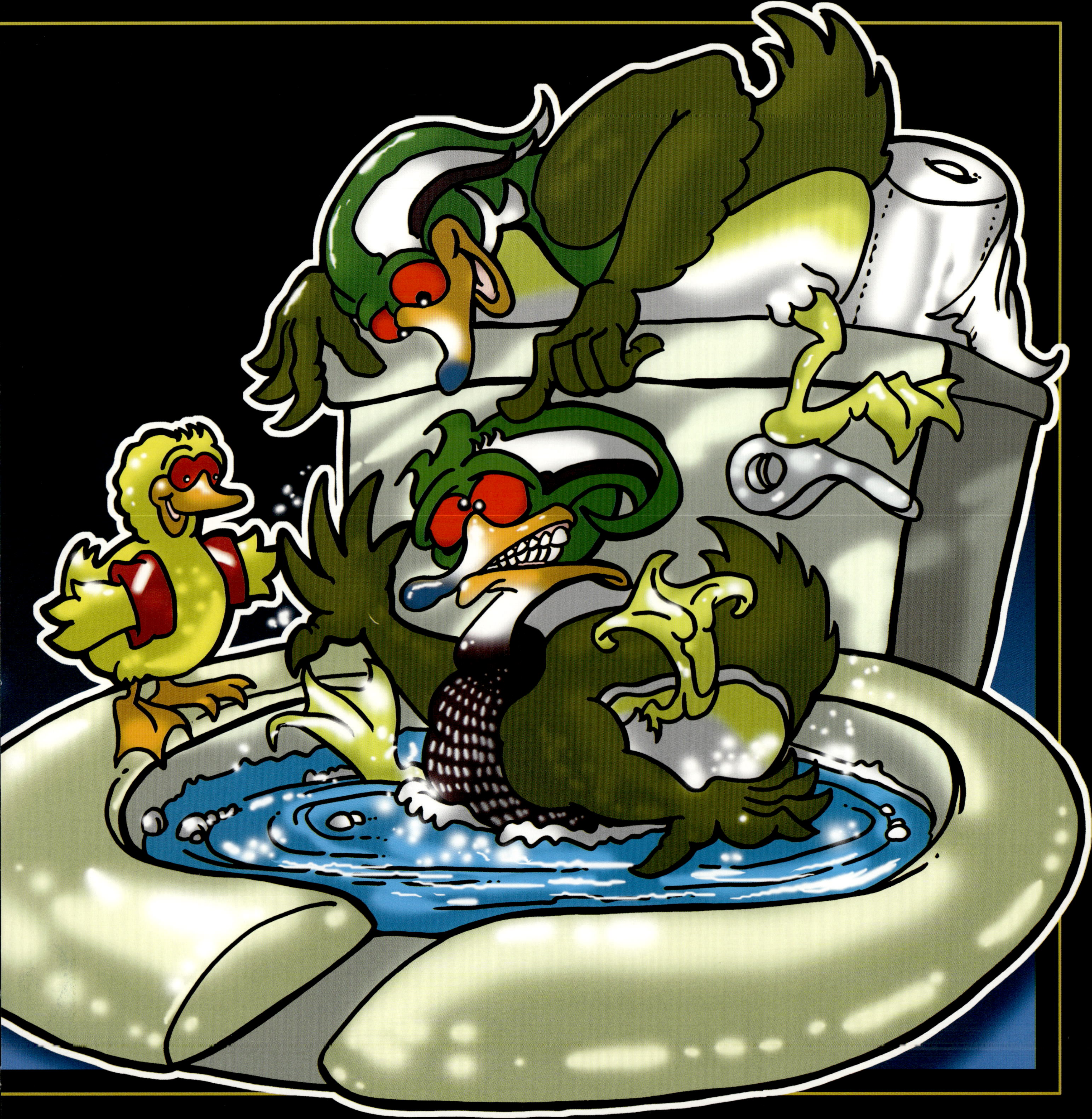

DIDYANO?

BE AWARE AND CARE

FLUSH of DUCKS
FAMILY: *ANATIDAE*

DUCKS are swimming birds that live near water. They have broad, flat bills, short legs, and oval bodies. They *waddle* instead of walking because of their webbed feet that they use like paddles. **Ducks** do not have nerves or blood vessels in their feet which mean they can swim in icy cold water or walk on frozen ponds. **Ducks** were the first birds recorded by the ancient Chinese to be tamed or *domesticated* by man.

Did you know **Ducks** nest in a family group called a *flush*? Sometimes **Ducks** are frightened and get *flushed* from their hiding places. **Wood Ducks** are colorful, North American **Ducks** that live in wooded swamps and streams. Many people consider them to be the most beautiful of all waterfowl. **Ducks'** feathers are waterproof. There is a special gland that produces oil near the tail that spreads and covers the outer coat of feathers. Beneath this waterproof layer are fluffy and soft feathers called *down* to keep them warm. **Ducks** keep clean by *preening* themselves with their bills, which they do often. They also line their nests with feathers pulled or *plucked* from their chest.

The *Spanish* word for **Duck** is *Pato*.

The male **Wood Duck** is called a *Drake*. He can measure up to 21 inches tall, weighing up to 30 ounces and have a wingspan of nearly 29 inches. The *Drake* is noted for his large crest and black, chestnut, green, purple, and white feathers or plumage.

The female **Wood Duck** is called a *Duck* or *Hen*. She is dull gray and brown and builds her nests in hollow trees or nesting boxes called *duck boxes*.

A baby **Wood Duck** is called a *Duckling* or *Flapper*. **Ducklings** may jump from their nests without injury. These nests can be as high as 90 feet in a tree.

Other family group names are: **Badelynge**, **Bunch**, **Brace**, **Flock**, **Gaggle**, **Paddling**, **Team**, **Raft**, **Badling**, **Bunch**, **Sord**, or **Waddling**.

The sound most **Ducks** make is called a *Quack*. When disturbed, a female **Wood Duck** makes loud *oo-eek, oo-eek* sounds and takes flight. The *Drake* has a thin, rising and falling *zeeting* whistle.

To get your Ducks in a row means to get organized or plan how to get something done.

Be Aware & Care
Wood Ducks, considered agricultural pests, are often shot for sport. You can show you care and help protect the Wood Ducks by making others aware why it is important to protect the waters and nesting areas of these beautiful birds.

DIDYANO? Some Ducks can fly as many as 300 miles a day?

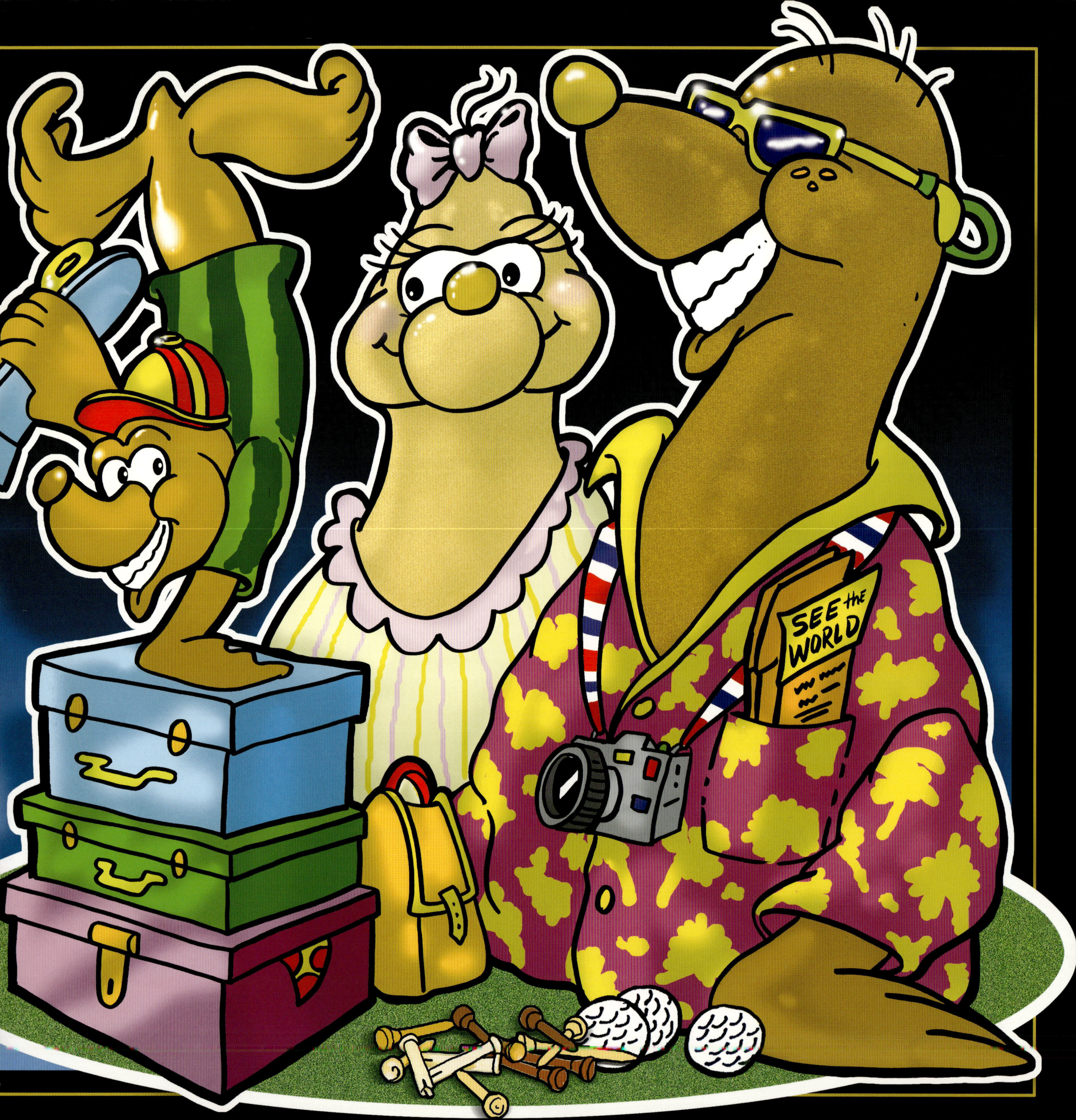
SEE the WORLD

DIDYANO?

BE AWARE AND CARE

TRIP of SEALS
FAMILY: *PHOCIDAE*

SEALS are marine mammals in the order **Pinnipedia**, which means *fin-footed*. They spend most of their lives in the sea, but also enjoy sunbathing on rocks or on the beach. The *Harbor Seal* lives along shorelines in the North Atlantic and Pacific Oceans. **Seals** have a life span of about 25 to 30 years.

Did you know **Seals** travel in a group called a *trip*? *Harbor Seals* take *trips* out to sea to hunt and feed. They spend about half their time on land and half in water. **Seals** sometimes sleep in the water. They can dive to 1,500 feet for as long as 40 minutes, although their average dive lasts three to seven minutes and is typically shallow. *Harbor Seals* generally do not touch each other when they exit the water or *haul out*. They maintain a space between themselves and other **Seals** of several feet or more. If touched by another **Seal**, they can get really angry!

Seals are different from *Sea Lions* mainly because **Seals** do not have ears on the outside of their heads. Also, **Seals** have shorter necks and short front or *fore flippers*. They also have claws on each toe on all four of their *flippers*.

The *Spanish* word for **Seal** is *Sellar* or *Foca*.

The male **Seal** is called a *Bull* or *Bachelor*. He can grow to be up to 6 feet long and can weigh as much as 375 pounds.

The female **Seal** is called a *Cow* or *Matka* and usually mates and gives birth once each year.

A baby **Seal** is called a *Pup* or *Weaner* and weighs about 30 pounds at birth. A *Pup* can swim at birth but will sometimes ride on its mother's back when it grows tired.

Other family group names are: **Pod**, **Herd**, **School**, **Rookery**, **Harem**, or **Team**.

The sound a **Seal** makes is called a *Bark*.

My lips are sealed doesn't mean my breath smells like fish. It means keeping a secret. It is something you say to let someone know you will not tell anyone else what he has just told you. *Get it?*

Be Aware & Care
Seals, like all marine mammals, are protected by the U.S. Marine Mammal Protection Act (MMPA) of 1972. You can show you care and help protect the Seals by making others aware that it is illegal to hunt or harass any marine mammal in U.S. waters.

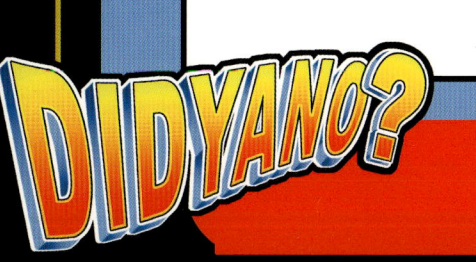

Seal teeth are black in color?

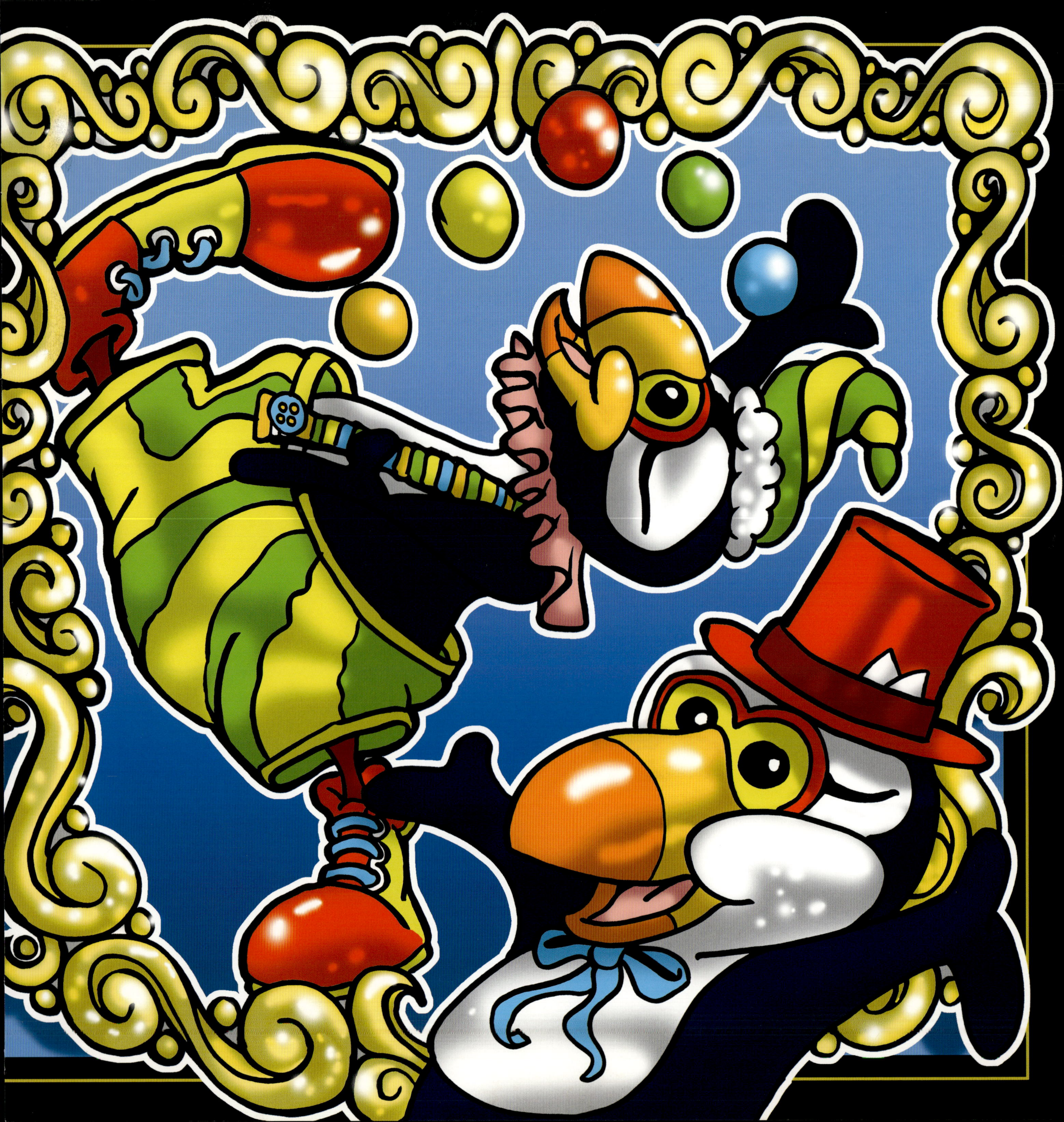

DIDYANO?

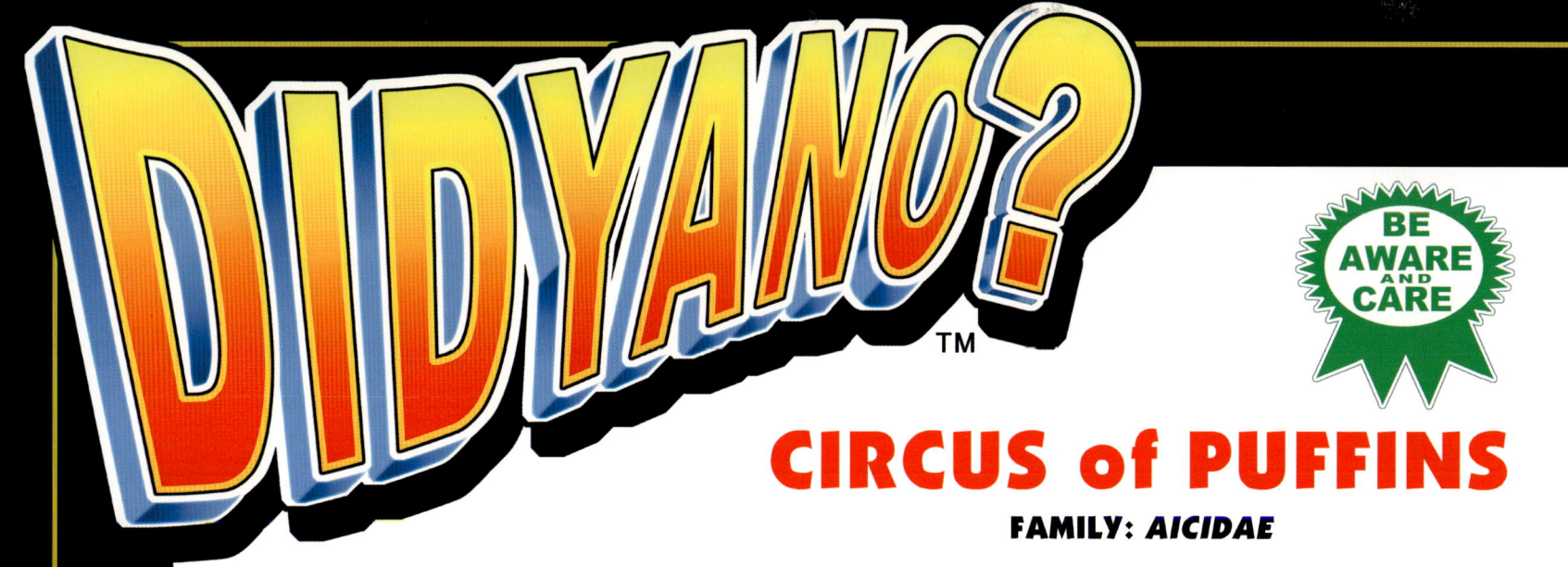

BE AWARE AND CARE

CIRCUS of PUFFINS
FAMILY: *AICIDAE*

PUFFINS are sometimes called *the clowns of the sea* because they are comical looking birds that look as if they are wearing too much makeup. **Puffins** have funny little bodies and waddle around, jumping from rock to rock. They are pudgy birds with short, red legs, black coloring on their backs and white on their bellies. Their faces are white and they have yellow eyes with red circles around them. The **Puffin's** bill is triangular in shape and colored red, orange and yellow.

Did you know **Puffins** nest in a group called a *circus*? **Puffins** look like little *circus* clowns all painted up and ready to perform a *circus act*. They usually lay only one egg in a nest which is typically a hole in the ground. Their food includes small fish, shellfish, and shrimp. **Puffins** fly very fast and are excellent swimmers and divers. **Puffins** have been known to dive over 200 feet under the water using their wings and webbed feet to swim. Mom and Dad **Puffins** rub their bills together to show affection. This is called *billing*.

The *Spanish* word for **Puffin** is *Frailecillo*. The *Latin* words **Fratercula Arctica** means *little brother of the north*.

The male **Puffin** is called a *Cock*. He stands 12 inches tall and weighs about 1 pound.

The female **Puffin** is called a *Hen* and can hold up to twelve small fish in her mouth at one time.

A baby **Puffin** is called a *Chick* or *Puffling*. **Puffin** originally meant *fatling* to describe the chubby chicks.

Other family group names are: **Colony** or **Pack**.

The sound a **Puffin** makes is called a *Growl*.

When someone says that *you eat like a bird*, they usually mean that you eat very little, but most birds can eat up to eight times their body weight in insects. **Puffins** eat up to six times their weight in fish.

If someone tells you a secret, and you don't want to tell who told it to you, you can just say *a little bird told you*. If a **Puffin** tries to whisper a secret in your ear, be very careful. They are known to bite very hard!

Be Aware & Care
Natural predators of the Puffins include Gulls, Sharks, and Killer Whales. Humans have hunted Puffins to near extinction in some areas. You can show you care and help protect the Puffins by making others aware that it is illegal to transport, sell or take the eggs of Puffins or bother their nests or nesting areas.

DIDYANO? Puffins can stand on their tippy-toes?

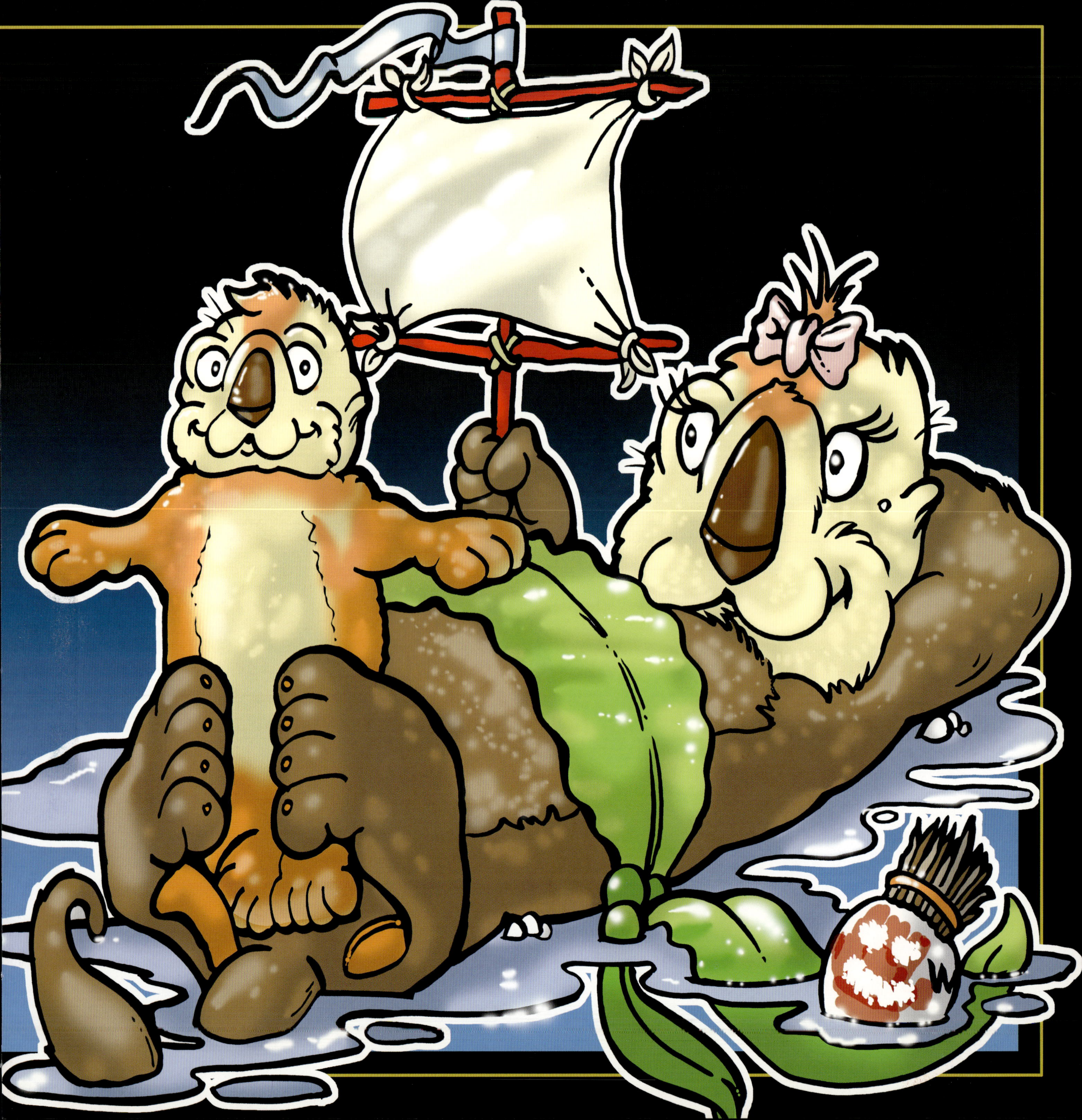

DIDYANO?

RAFT of SEA OTTERS
FAMILY: *MUSTELIDAE*

BE AWARE AND CARE

SEA OTTERS are sleek, thick furred, marine mammals that live along rocky Pacific Ocean coasts around areas of seaweed called *kelp beds*. They spend their entire life in the water and have large, webbed, hind feet which they use to swim. Their forefeet are smaller and they use rocks to help crack open their favorite foods: *clams*, *crabs*, *sea urchins* and *abalone*. Adult **Sea Otters** can hold their breath for as long as eight minutes while diving to the ocean floor in search of food. **Sea Otters** have the thickest fur of any marine mammal, averaging 650,000 hairs per square inch!

Did you know **Sea Otters** are often seen floating on the water like little boats or *rafts*? They lay on their backsides with all four paws out of the water sunbathing and cleaning their fur. At night they anchor themselves to a piece of *kelp* by wrapping up in the leaves to sleep, floating to-and-fro so they won't drift away with the currents. Sometimes they hold onto each other as they sleep.

The *Spanish* word for Otter is *Nutria marina* and *Nutria del Kamtchatka*.

The male **Sea Otter** is called a *Sire*. He will grow to about 4 feet long and can weigh between 65 to 80 pounds. The **Sea Otter** is considered one of the smallest of all marine mammals.

The female **Sea Otter** is called a *Dame*. She wraps her young in *kelp leaves* when leaving to go hunting so they don't wander or drift off.

A baby **Sea Otter** is called a *Pup*, *Cub*, *Kitten* or *Whelp* and will weigh 3-5 pounds at birth. The *Pup* rides around on mom's belly as she *rafts* around on her back. Mom and baby play in the water and nap in the sun together. Unlike their cousin the **River Otter**, the **Sea Otter** *Pup* is born with its eyes open. Also, the **River Otter** is born in a den called a *holt*, while the **Sea Otter** gives birth in the water.

Other family group names are: *Romp*, *Bevy*, *Lodge*, or *Family*.

A **Sea Otter** makes many sounds. It *Whistles*, *Growls*, *Screams*, *Barks*, *Chirps*, or *Coos*.

Be Aware & Care
Sea Otters were once abundant along most of the coastal North Pacific Ocean. That was before fur traders hunted them for their thick, luxurious pelts. By the year 1900, Sea Otters were nearly extinct. You can show you care and help protect the Sea Otters by making others aware that their biggest problem is man and pollution, especially the effects of an oil spill. If a Sea Otter swims into an oil spill, its fur becomes soiled and loses its ability to keep the cold water from getting to its skin, causing hypothermia and ultimately, death.

Sea Otters carry around their favorite rock to crack open food?

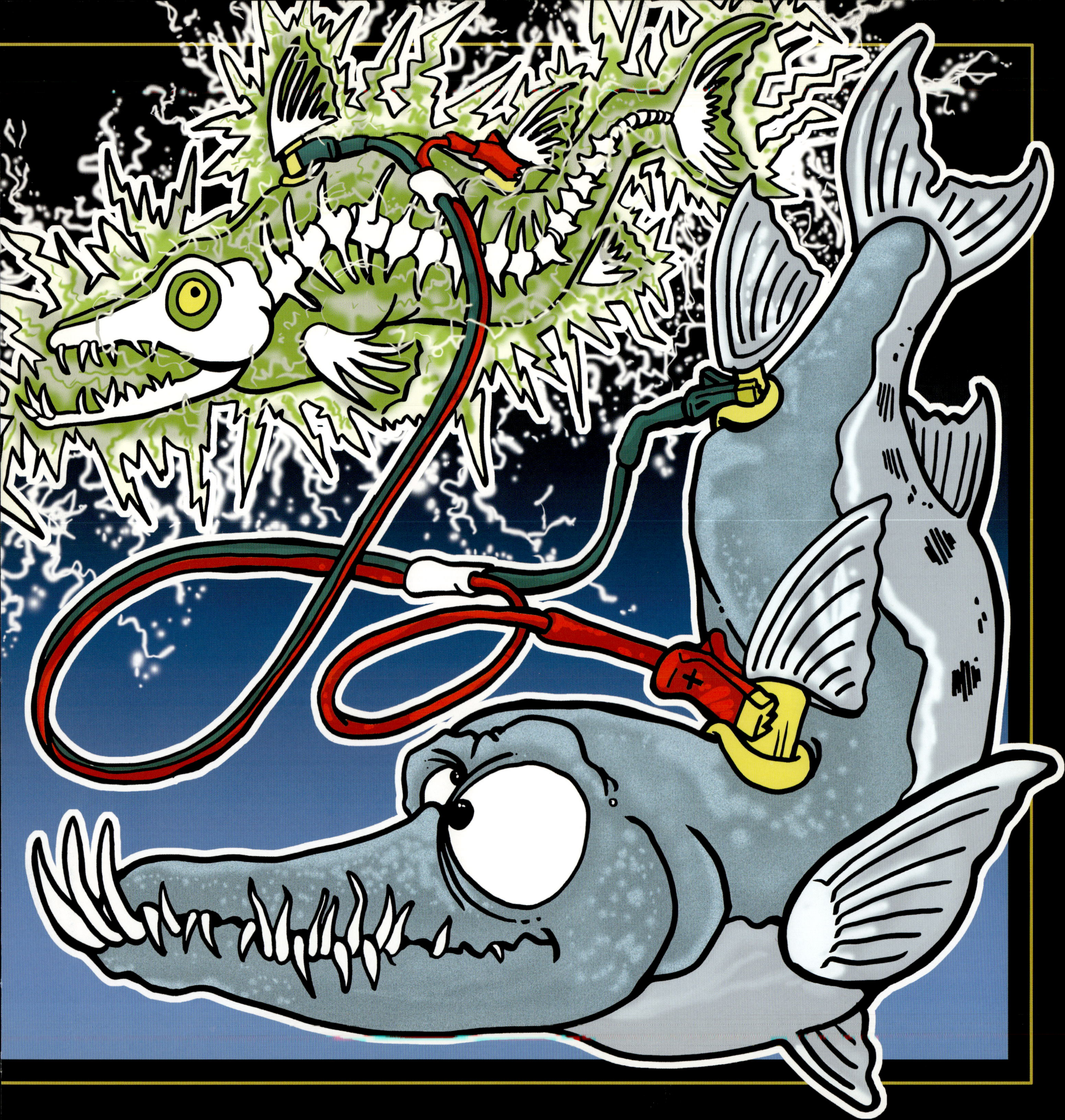

DIDYANO?

BE AWARE AND CARE

BATTERY of BARRACUDAS
FAMILY: *SPHYRAENIDAE*

BARRACUDAS are swift and powerful fish with long bodies, two different top fins or *dorsal fins*, and large heads with big eyes. They have a large mouth, jutting lower jaw, and long, sharp teeth to slice their victims to pieces. **Barracudas** can lay motionless in the water, hovering around reefs with their mouths half open. Seeing an unsuspecting fish swimming by, the **Barracudas** shoot forward as fast as a silver bullet, catching their prey.

Did you know **Barracudas** gather in a huge group of several thousand called a *battery*? A *battery* is any large group or series of related things like a *battery of questions*. **Barracudas** are called the *Tigers of the Sea* and are usually found in warm, tropical regions.

In order to move up and down quickly to track its prey and move around the coral reefs, the **Barracuda** uses its *swim bladder*. A **Barracuda** can inflate or deflate this gas-filled chamber to raise or lower its body in the water. A *swim bladder* keeps a fish from sinking to the bottom of the ocean, even though its body is heavier than seawater.

The *Spanish* word for **Barracuda** is *Barraco* meaning *Overlapping Tooth* or *Snaggle-Toothed*.

The male **Barracuda** is called a *Bruiser* and has been recorded to reach 6 feet in length and weigh 85 pounds.

The female **Barracuda** is called a *Butch*. She does not care for her young when they are born.

A young **Barracuda** is called a *Spet* or *Cuda* and has a long dark stripe across its body. As it grows, the stripe breaks up, becoming blotched and eventually it disappears.

Other family group names are: *School*, *Shoal*, *Draft*, *Nest*, *Cast*, *Draught*, *Run*, *Catch*, *Drift*, or *Haul*.

The sound a **Barracuda** makes is called a … well, they don't make any sounds because they are quiet hunters. Maybe they make a *wooshing* sound as they rush through the water after their prey.

Few people would think twice about kissing a **Barracuda**, despite the fact that most brands of lipsticks contain fish scales.

Be Aware & Care
Many species of Barracuda are classified as game fish and are considered of minor commercial importance. You can show you care and help protect the Barracuda by making others aware that eating Barracuda is much more harmful to humans than eating most any other fish species. Explain to your family and friends that people sometimes become ill or sick from *ciguatera fish poisoning* after eating Barracuda.

Barracudas can swim after their prey at over 40 feet per second?

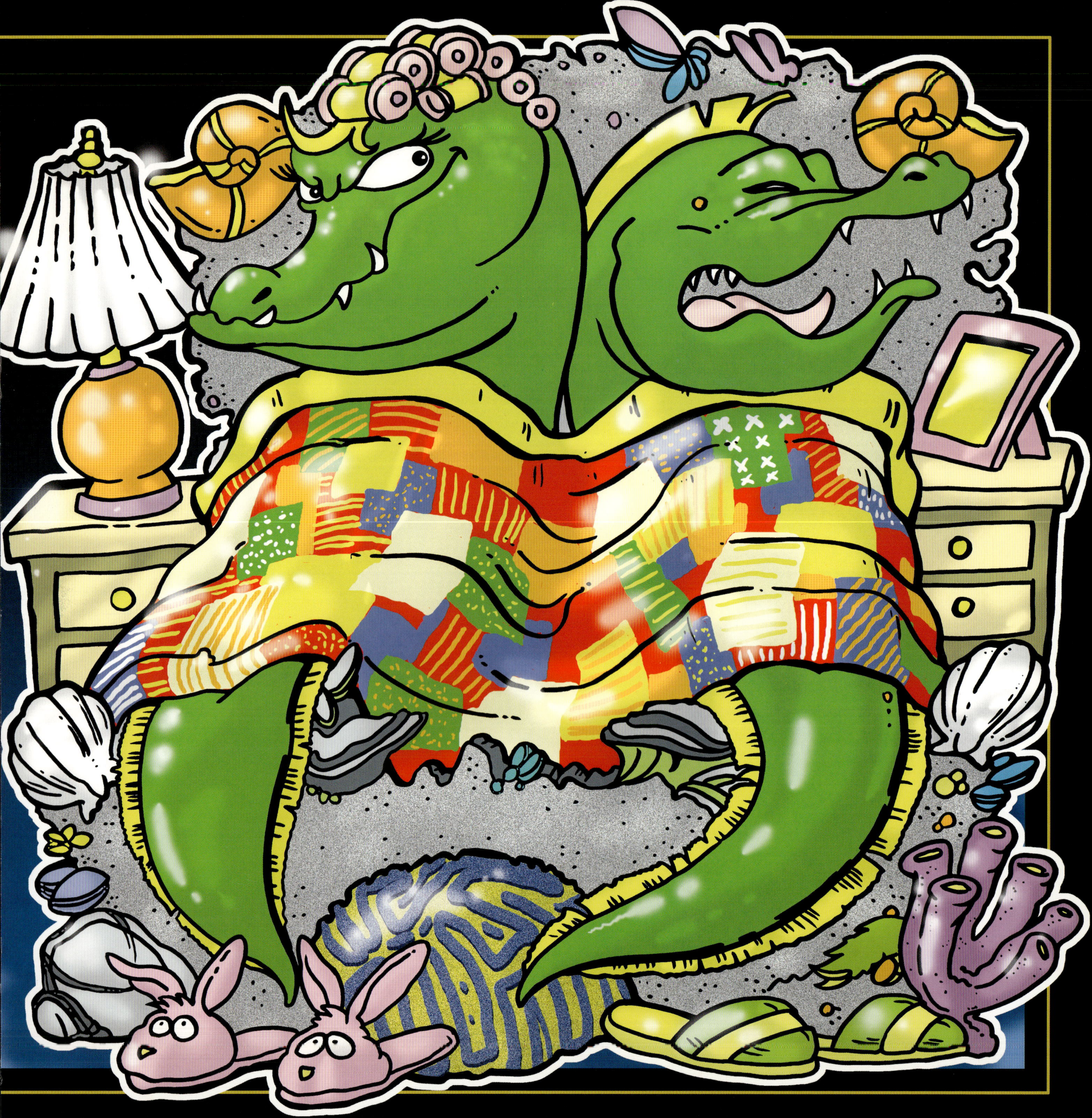

DIDYANO? ™

BED of EELS
FAMILY: *MURAENIDAE*

BE AWARE AND CARE

MORAY EELS are long, slender animals that live in saltwater and usually around reefs. **Green Moray Eels** are actually blue, but have a slimy yellow coating on their bodies that makes them appear green. The slime protects these common tropical **Eels** as they wiggle through jagged coral. **Moray Eels** appear very dangerous because they are always opening and closing their mouths, showing their mean looking teeth. This action is not really bad, but simply the way they breathe. **Moray Eels** have two sets of jaws; one in their mouths, and one inside their throats.

Did you know **Moray Eels** gather together in a group called a *bed*? They rest in their *beds* by day in holes within the reefs and come out at night to feed. **Moray Eels** have large mouths and powerful jaws with a vice-like grip. They have sharp teeth that protrude from the upper and lower jaws, and sometimes from the roof of their mouths. The teeth of **Moray Eels** point backwards to prevent slippery prey like fish and octopus from escaping their bite.

The *Spanish* word for **Eel** is *Anguilla*.

The male **Moray Eel** is simply called a *Male* and can grow to be 15 feet long.

The female **Moray Eel** is simply called a *Female*. She lays clear eggs in the open water. Each egg has a tiny *larva* inside it. As the *larva* grows, its body changes shape into a tiny eel that is nearly see-through like glass. This clear eel is called a *glass eel*.

A baby **Moray Eel** is called a *Fly* or *Elver*. After it hatches from its egg, it starts to swim and feed on its own immediately.

Other family group names are: **Swarm**, **Draft**, **Wisp**, or **Knot**.

The sound an **Eel** makes is called a *Chomp*.

If someone you know is as *slippery as an Eel*, then he is someone who is devious and cannot be trusted. He could also be as *crooked as an Eel*.

Be Aware & Care
Moray Eels are not currently threatened. You can show you care and help protect the Moray Eels by making others aware why it is important to protect the waters and coral reefs Eels live in. Explain to your family and friends that Moray Eels are feared for their vicious bite. However, it is worth noting that they rarely bite unless provoked.

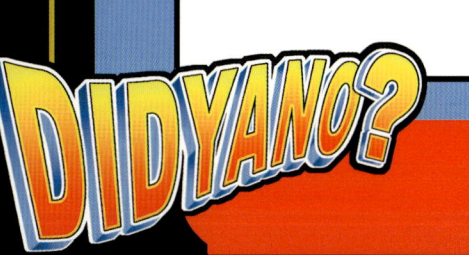

DIDYANO?
Moray Eels have two sets of jaws?

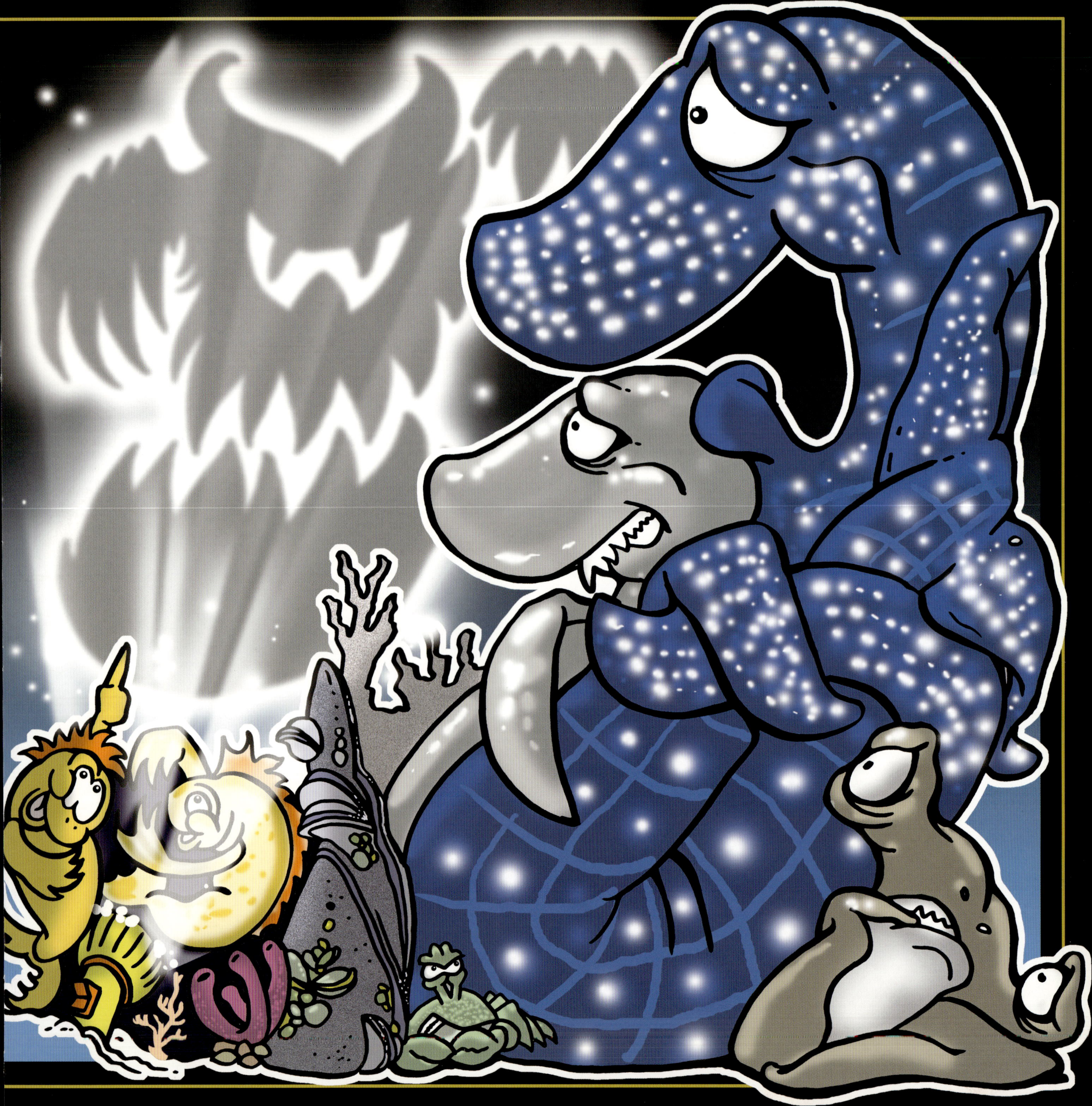

DIDYANO?

BE AWARE AND CARE

SHIVER of SHARKS
FAMILY: *RHINCODONTIDAE*

SHARKS are fish with powerful, streamlined bodies. There are more than 340 known species of Sharks. They breathe underwater using *gill slits* and have replaceable teeth in case they lose any. Sharks have no bones in their bodies; their skeletons are made up of *cartilage*. Many Sharks, like the *Great White*, eat meat, fish, and seals and will grow about 10 inches per year. The largest of all the Sharks is the *Whale Shark* which feeds mainly on *plankton*. *Plankton* is made up of tiny plants and animals. The word *plankton* comes from the Greek word *planktos* which means *drifting*.

Did you know that Sharks swim in a group called a *shiver*? It is believed sailors of old witnessed great schools of man-eaters like *Hammerhead Sharks* circling below their ships. It gave them the *shivers* knowing what would happen if they fell overboard!

The *Spanish* word for Shark is *Tiburon* and for Whale Shark is *Tiburon ballena*.

The male Whale Shark is called a *Bull* and has been recorded at almost 42 feet long, 23 feet wide, and weighing more than 47,000 pounds. It is the world's biggest fish. A Whale Shark has approximately 300 rows of teeth, with hundreds of tiny teeth in each row. Its skin, blue-gray in color, has a unique combination of white spots and stripes.

The female Whale Shark is called a *Nurse*. A Whale Shark mom can carry up to 300 eggs at a time and each egg case can be 14 inches long. The babies remain inside the egg cases and inside mom until they are fully developed.

A baby Whale Shark is called a *Pup*. When the *Pup* is old enough and large enough to survive on its own, mom releases it and the others into the open ocean. Each *Pup* can be 2 feet long when released.

Other family group names are: School or Shoal.

The sound a Shark makes is called a *Belch*.

Dried *Shark skin* called shagreen was used in the past as sandpaper. In Germany and Japan, *Shark skin* was used on sword handles for a non-slip grip.

Be Aware & Care
In some countries, Whale Sharks are hunted for their hides and for food. You can show you care and help protect the Whale Sharks by making others aware that one of the biggest threats to a Whale Shark is being hit by boats as they feed. Explain to your family and friends that Whale Sharks are protected against the threat of fishing in the southeastern waters of the United States, but not everywhere else in the world.

The Whale Shark is the world's biggest fish?

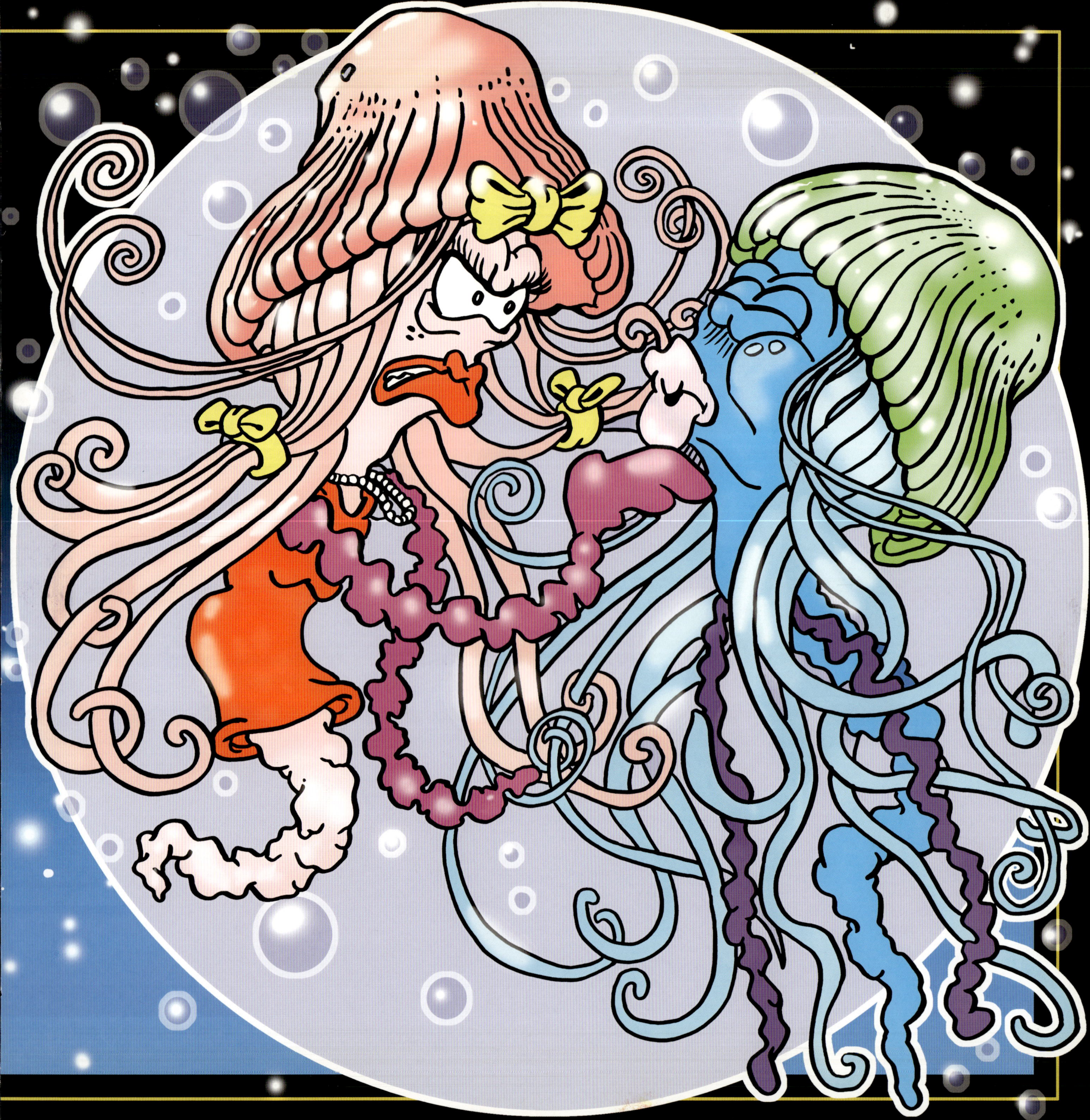

DIDYANO?

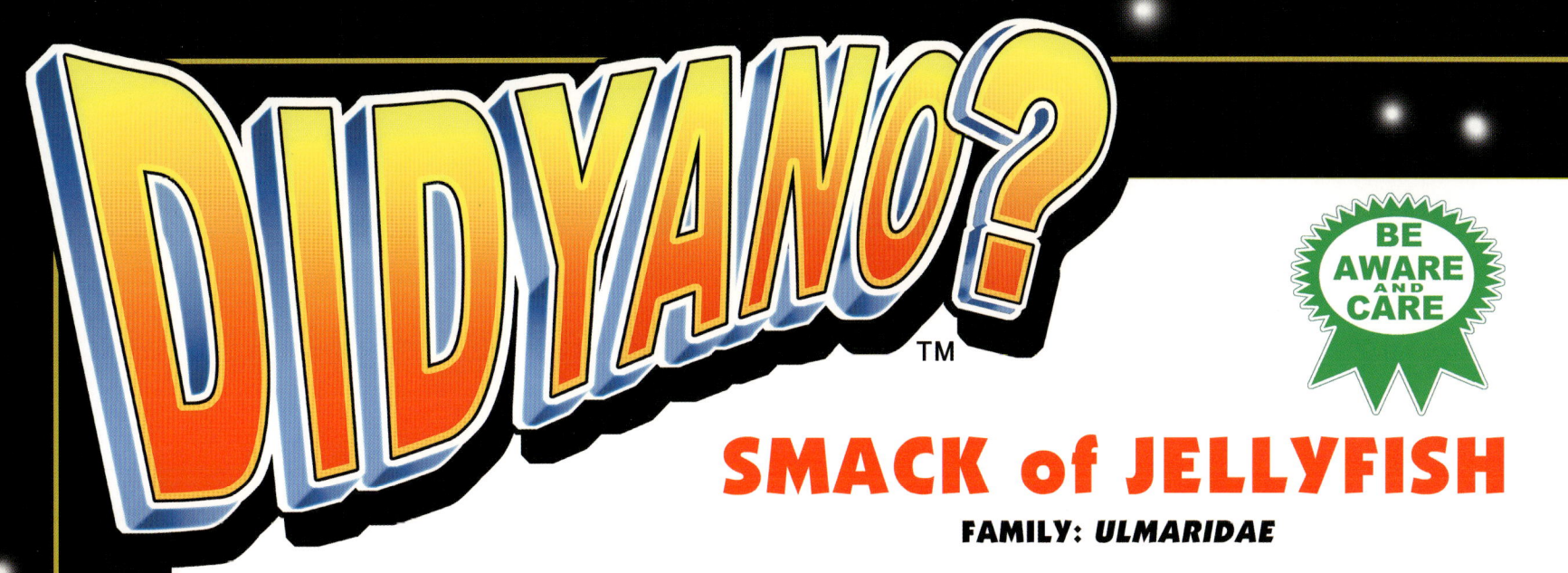

SMACK of JELLYFISH
FAMILY: *ULMARIDAE*

BE AWARE AND CARE

JELLYFISH have long, soft bodies and poisonous, stinging arms or *tentacles* which they use to catch fish. Their bodies are made up of two layers with a *jellylike* substance in between. Their bodies are shaped like a bell and may be nearly clear or have colors such as pale blue, orange, brown, white or pink. Some Jellyfish even glow in the dark. Jellyfish are made up of 98% water and can range in size from a few inches to over three feet across. The largest Jellyfish is the *Lion's Mane*. Their *tentacles* can reach up to 120 feet in length.

Did you know that Jellyfish travel in a group called a *smack*? A *smack* was a type of sailing boat used to transport fish to market. Smacks have large round sails and usually travel together in a close group.

Jellyfish float in the sea, spreading their stinging *tentacles*. For the Jellyfish, movement is quite hard. There is a ring of muscles around the base of their bodies called the *umbrella* or *bell*, which has to squeeze water out to move the Jellyfish forward. When they get near a fish, they will sting it, catch it and eat it. Even humans can feel the sting of the Jellyfish. Although most Jellyfish poisons are not deadly to humans, the sting of the *Box Jellyfish* can kill a man. The *Sea Wasp*, a type of Jellyfish, is the world's most deadly creature.

The *Spanish* word for Jellyfish is *Medusa*.

The male Jellyfish is simply called a *Male*.

The female Jellyfish is simply called a *Female*. She releases many *larvae* into the water that attach themselves to the oceans bottom where they develop into *polyps*.

A baby Jellyfish, called an *Ephyna*, comes from the *polyp* when it breaks apart.

Other family group names are: **Brood**, **Smuth**, **Smuck**, or **Fluther**.

The sound Jellyfish make is called a *Scream*. Jellyfish themselves don't make sounds, but if they sting you at the beach, that's what you'll hear!

Be Aware & Care
Jellyfish are not threatened or endangered. On the contrary, scientists seem to think there has been an increase in the Jellyfish population over the last decade. There is speculation that this may be due to the decreasing populations of major predators such as Sea Turtles and Tuna. You can show you care and help by making others aware why it is important to protect the predators that feed on Jellyfish and keep their numbers under control. Tell your friends that polluting our oceans is also a serious problem, to not only the Jellyfish, but to all the sea creatures.

DIDYANO?
Jellyfish do not have hearts or brains?

DIDYANO?™

Animal Families of the Zoos & Aquariums

Written and Illustrated by
Timothy D. Thomas

AQUARIUMS

Did you know the word **Aqua** means *water*? The term **Aquarium** is defined as a place for the public exhibition of live aquatic plants and animals. An **Aquarium** or ***Marine Park*** is a place or facility where fish, plants and other living animals, especially wild ones, are kept within enclosures and displayed for people to see and admire.

The staff and workers of **Aquariums** do more than just display wild animals.

- They watch and observe the animals for scientific research and study.
- They promote public education and awareness about different kinds of wild animals and their natural habitats.
- They observe living, eating and mating habits of the animals and how their babies are born and raised.
- They take care of sick, injured or orphaned animals.
- And much, much more!

Other names for **Aquariums** are:
Marine Parks or ***Water Parks***.

Thank you to The Association of Zoos and Aquariums (AZA) and the Alliance for Marine Mammal Parks and Aquariums (AMMPA) for their input and review of the contents of this book.

This book is dedicated to all the people who work to make visiting Zoos and Aquariums a pleasant experience for us all!

A Special Thank You

Terri, Tanis, Mark, Vivian, Herb, Dewey, Kathy,
Kevin, Gwen, Missi, Miki, Lydia, Ed
and all my family & friends for their support!

Disclaimer:

*DIDYANO? is an educational resource written for elementary age students. Thomas Expressions, LLC. does not cover all species in their entirety, nor are we capable of including all the latest scientific information and facts about the animals described.
Though we edit our accounts for accuracy, we cannot guarantee all information in those accounts. While Thomas Expressions, LLC. 's staff and contributors provide reputable information, we cannot necessarily endorse the contents of references beyond our control.*

Thank you.

Endangered Species Terms

Vulnerable Species
A species particularly at risk because of low or declining numbers or small range, but not a threatened species.

Threatened Species
A species whose population is not yet low enough to be in immediate danger of extinction, but which certainly faces serious problems. If the problems affecting these species aren't resolved, it is probable that the species will become endangered. The Eastern Indigo Snake and the Red Kangaroo are examples of threatened species.

Endangered Species
A species, plant or animal, that is in immediate danger of becoming extinct. Its numbers are usually low, and it needs protection in order to survive. The Siberian Tiger, the Southern Sea Otter, the Snow Leopard, the Green Pitcher Plant, and thousands of other plants and animals are endangered worldwide.

Extinct Species
An extinct species is one that is no longer living. The Passenger Pigeon, the Dodo, and the Stegosaurus are examples of extinct species. These animals no longer exist on the earth.

DID YOU KNOW

DIDYANO?

Animal Families of the Zoos & Aquariums

_____
THIS BOOK BELONGS TO

_____
FROM

_____
DATE

BE AWARE AND CARE

Written and Illustrated by
Timothy D. Thomas